# be a
# beautiful
# bride

hamlyn

# be a
# beautiful
# bride

Veronique Henderson
Pat Henshaw

with colour**me**beautiful

DEDICATION
To Jim and John

An Hachette UK Company
www.hachette.co.uk

First published in Great Britain in 2009 by
Hamlyn, a division of Octopus Publishing Group Ltd
2–4 Heron Quays, London E14 4JP
www.octopusbooksusa.com

This edition published in 2010

Distributed in the U.S. and Canada by Octopus Books USA:
c/o Hachette Book Group
237 Park Avenue
New York NY 10017

Every effort has been made to reproduce the colors in this book
accurately; however, the printing process can lead to some
discrepancies. The color samples provided should be used as
a guideline only.

ISBN 978-0-600-62026-6

Printed and bound in China

10 9 8 7 6 5 4 3 2 1

# Contents

INTRODUCTION  6

1 all about color 8

2 shapes and styles 38

3 completing the look 74

4 the bridal party 94

5 looking great on your big day 114

INDEX  126

ACKNOWLEDGMENTS  128

# introduction

CONGRATULATIONS! YOU ARE EMBARKING ON AN EXCITING JOURNEY, AND WE WANT TO HELP YOU MAKE YOUR WEDDING DAY A MOST MEMORABLE AND BEAUTIFUL ONE. WITH SO MUCH TO THINK ABOUT AND SO MUCH INFORMATION AVAILABLE, OUR AIM IS TO GUIDE YOU TOWARD THE RIGHT CHOICE OF DRESS FOR *YOU*, AS WELL AS THROUGH A WHOLE HOST OF OTHER DECISIONS YOU WILL NEED TO MAKE.

## your big day

Experts are available to help you with wedding etiquette, the type of ceremony you might choose, and even the vows you can make. This book focuses on how you can look your very best on your wedding day. It will help you decide what you and your bridal party should wear, as you will be the center of everyone's attention. This is *your* day, and by understanding yourself and what suits you, you will be able to make your own decisions about what you want to wear and do on your special day. This book is not intended to be prescriptive, because every bride will have her individual personality and her own thoughts about her ideal bridal gown.

You may have dreamed about your wedding day and what you want (and don't want) to wear, although sometimes dreams are simply not realistic. However, this book will show you how to make those dreams as much of a reality as possible, by helping you focus on those things that will make you a truly beautiful bride, completely confident and comfortable in what you are wearing. In the chapters that follow, we will show you:

- The right colors for your complexion.
- The right dress styles for your body shape.
- How to coordinate your look with makeup, hairstyling, and accessories that suit your face shape, scale, and proportions. Remember that your partner is marrying you, not someone he fails to recognize on the day.
- How to ensure that your bridal party coordinates with you.
- And finally, how to make your wedding day simply the best.

all about color

# considering color

IN THE WESTERN WORLD, TRADITIONALLY BRIDES WEAR A VIRGINAL PURE WHITE. OVER THE YEARS, HOWEVER, CONVENTIONS HAVE CHANGED. THE AVERAGE AGE OF A BRIDE IS NOW 31 YEARS AND 6 MONTHS, AND THE NATURE OF MANY WEDDINGS HAS BEEN TRANSFORMED TO ALLOW A MORE FLEXIBLE CHOICE OF COLORS AND STYLES. IN SOME CULTURES, COLORFUL WEDDING DRESSES ARE THE NORM, BUT YOU STILL NEED TO MAKE SURE THAT THE ONE YOU CHOOSE IS THE RIGHT SHADE FOR YOU.

## the importance of color

Many brides will still choose to wear a "white" dress. However, at **colour me beautiful** we know that there are many shades of white, cream and ivory. So, it is not just a matter of choosing a "white" dress, but a "white" that is right for your coloring. This will depend on your skin tone, eye, and hair color.

Any color you wear near your face will reflect upward onto it. If the color is in harmony and balance with your natural coloring, you will look healthier and more radiant. If the color is wrong, it can create shadows, dark circles around your eyes, and even give you an uneven complexion, which you may then need to cover with heavier makeup.

are: Light, Deep, Warm, Cool, Clear, or Soft. You can then use this knowledge to help you select a color for your wedding dress, as well as colors to use as accents for flowers, trims, jewelry, and even shoes.

## changing colors

Before you establish your coloring, you will need to decide what you want to do with your hair color (see Tips for the Day on pages 12–17), since this may change your overall appearance. You may even be considering tinted contact lenses, which will also affect your overall appearance. However, be aware that drastic changes may not always work successfully or look natural.

**ABOVE** *Here we see a bride with warm coloring wearing pure white, which is hard and harsh against her skin tone.*

**LEFT** *A warm cream-toned wedding dress complements the creamy skin tones of this warm bride.*

Over many years, **colour me beautiful** has developed an extensive color system, but for this book we have chosen to use just six dominant coloring types. If you find that you do not fit exactly into one of these, you may benefit from a detailed personal analysis from a professional consultant.

## what is color?

All colors are made up of three elements:

**Depth (light to dark)** In other words, how much white there is in a color—lack of white in a color deepens its shade and tone.

**Undertone (warm or cool)** This denotes how much yellow or blue there is in a color—for more warmth, add yellow; to cool it down, add blue.

**Clarity (clear to soft)** Clear colors are vibrant and intense, soft colors muted and dusty. Over the following pages you will be able to identify which of the six dominant **colour me beautiful** coloring types you

### ALTERNATIVE ADVICE

The advice we give on color applies not only to a traditional wedding dress but also to any alternative outfit you may choose to wear (see pages 68–71). Remember to take a look at bridesmaids' dresses, too. Many of these would make a beautiful wedding dress and may be available in exactly the color you want.

# light

CHOOSING A WEDDING DRESS IS EASY FOR A BRIDE WITH LIGHT COLORING. YOUR DELICATE COLORING WILL BE PERFECTLY BALANCED AND COMPLEMENTED BY ALL SHADES OF WHITE AND CREAM. IF YOU CHOOSE TO USE COLOR, YOU SHOULD STICK TO LIGHT AND PASTEL SHADES NEAR YOUR FACE.

## do you have...

- Naturally blond hair with light eyebrows and lashes?
- Pale, light-colored eyes?
- Delicate porcelain skin?

## the light bride

Your overall look is light and delicate, so you are going to look wonderful in all the traditional whites, ivories, and creams. Pastels and light colors will also work well. You do not want to be overwhelmed by strong coloring, worn by either yourself or any of the wedding party who might be standing near you. The groom can also lighten his look, even if he is wearing a dark suit.

**ABOVE** *Ulrika Jonsson has typical light coloring; the soft white color and delicate fabric of her dress balance with her coloring.*

### TIPS FOR THE DAY

- If you want to enhance your hair color, golden or ash highlights are your best choices.
- Your skin tone is delicate, so don't hide it under a fake or real tan.

## ACCENT COLORS

| DUSTY ROSE | BLUSH PINK | GERANIUM | VIOLET | APPLE GREEN | PRIMROSE | LIGHT AQUA | SKY BLUE |

# deep

AS A DEEP BRIDE YOU WILL NEED TO THINK CAREFULLY ABOUT YOUR
COLOR CHOICES TO ENSURE THAT YOU MAKE THE MOST OF YOUR
FABULOUS LOOK. CHOOSING THE RIGHT LIGHT SHADE FOR YOU IS VERY
IMPORTANT—HAVE FUN TEAMING IT WITH COLORFUL ACCESSORIES
AND MAKEUP.

## do you have...
- Dark hair?
- Dark eyes?
- Porcelain to dark skin?

## the deep bride

On your wedding day you
want to look stunning, and if
you choose to wear a light-
colored dress you will need to
balance it with rich tones in
your makeup and accent colors.
Your natural coloring will
always be best in darker, stronger
colors. By being creative and
bringing more color into your
look, perhaps with trims or
accessories, you will be able to
create a dramatic look.

**ABOVE** *Jennifer Lopez has stunning
dark eyes and beautiful dark hair;
the low neckline of her dress works
well with her coloring.*

## TIPS FOR THE DAY
- Don't be tempted to highlight your
hair—just keep it in good condition
to make it shine.
- Make sure your foundation
matches your skin tone perfectly
to avoid a masklike appearance.

## ACCENT COLORS

| SCARLET | BITTERSWEET | TURQUOISE | ROYAL PURPLE | FOREST | TRUE BLUE | BURGUNDY | BLACK |
|---------|-------------|-----------|--------------|--------|-----------|----------|-------|

# warm

WARM BRIDES OFTEN HAVE VERY PALE PORCELAIN SKIN THAT IS BEST
COMPLEMENTED WITH IVORY OR CREAM SHADES. IF YOU HAVE ANY
FRECKLES, DON'T TRY TO HIDE THEM, ALONG WITH THE RED TONES
IN YOUR HAIR, THEY WILL BALANCE BEAUTIFULLY WITH COLORS THAT
HAVE A YELLOW UNDERTONE.

## do you have...

- Any shade of red hair, from
  auburn to strawberry blond?
- Brown, hazel, green, or blue eyes?
- Golden or freckled skin?

## the warm bride

Your wonderful warm coloring
will be enhanced by all the
fantastic ivories, creams, and
golden shades. If you choose
o wear a pure white dress,
adding texture, embroidery, or
lace will soften the look of the
fabric to balance your skin tone.
Golden jewelry will be your
best choice, and your makeup
colors will need to be yellow-
based to coordinate with your
overall look.

**ABOVE** *Sarah Ferguson wore a
beautifully embellished cream dress,
decorated with pearls, and had
yellow flowers in her bouquet.*

## TIPS FOR THE DAY

- Enhancing the color of your hair
with gold tones will add to your
overall golden look.
- If you have freckles anywhere,
don't hide them—they are part
of who you are.

## ACCENT COLORS

| CORAL | TANGERINE | DAFFODIL | LIME | AQUA | MOSS | BRONZE | CHOCOLATE |

# cool

A BRIDE WITH COOL COLORING WILL LOOK GOOD IN PURE WHITE AND ALL SHADES OF IVORY. OTHER COLORS NEED TO HAVE A COOL OR BLUE TONE TO THEM. IF YOU ARE A COOL BRIDE YOU SHOULD MAKE THE MOST OF YOUR BEAUTIFUL EYES WITH SHADES OF MAKEUP THAT COMPLEMENT RATHER THAN DISTRACT.

## do you have...

- Ash tones or gray hair?
- Blue or gray eyes?
- Rosy skin tone?

## the cool bride

With your rosy skin tone you can balance your look with magnificent whites. You should avoid creamy yellows, but you can choose from all the icy shades, including hints of lavender as well as pinks, blues, and mints. Keeping your makeup colors cool-toned, will guarantee a flawless look. Think silver, platinum, and the biggest diamond he can afford!

**ABOVE** *The Duchess of Cornwall chose to wear a silvery-gray wedding dress that made the most of her cool coloring.*

### TIPS FOR THE DAY

- Don't try to hide any gray hair— just enhance it with ash-toned tints or highlights.
- Although your makeup colors should remain cool, avoid bright blue eye shadow if you have blue eyes.

## ACCENT COLORS

| BABY PINK | HOT PINK | PEPPERMINT | BRIGHT PERIWINKLE | BLUE-RED | SAPPHIRE | BLUEBELL | DUCK EGG |

# clear

IF YOU HAVE CLEAR COLORING, THE CONTRAST BETWEEN YOUR HAIR
COLOR, SKIN TONE, AND EYE COLOR NEEDS TO BE COMPLEMENTED
WITH COLORS THAT HAVE IMPACT. SO IF YOU CHOOSE TO WEAR ANY
SHADE OF WHITE OR CREAM, BALANCE IT WITH BRIGHTLY COLORED
FLOWERS OR ACCESSORIES.

## do you have...

• Dark hair?
• Bright blue, green, or topaz eyes?
• Pale porcelain skin?

## the clear bride

Your striking appearance is
best balanced with clear, bright
tones. If you choose to wear
white or ivory, a sheen on the
fabric will add to its clarity.
Your hair should give the light-
against-dark contrast that is
typical of your coloring, while
accent colors will do the same
against a pale dress.

**ABOVE** *Liz Hurley chose to wear
a bright pink dress to balance with
her dark hair, bright eyes, and
stunning clear look.*

## TIPS FOR THE DAY

• Stick to lowlights if you want to
enhance your hair color.
• If you need to wear glasses, make
sure you have nonreflective lenses
so that your eye makeup colors
show through.

## ACCENT COLORS

| BLUSH PINK | RUBY | LAPIS | PURPLE | CHINESE BLUE | LIGHT AQUA | LIGHT TEAL | EMERALD GREEN |

# soft

YOUR MUTED EYE COLORING, ALONG WITH THE BLENDED TONES IN
YOUR HAIR, GIVES YOU A CHOICE OF MANY COLORS THAT WILL LOOK
STUNNING ON YOU. SOFT WHITES AND CREAMS WILL BE GREAT FOR A
TRADITIONAL LOOK, AND TAUPES AND BEIGES ARE FANTASTIC FOR
SOMETHING A LITTLE DIFFERENT.

## do you have...

- Mousy hair, often highlighted?
- Blended, muted eye tone?
- Neutral skin tone?

## the soft bride

The fabulous softness of your
look needs to be balanced with
gentle tonal colors such as soft
whites, ivories, and champagne.
Your accent colors should be
more tonal than high contrast.
Fabric with texture will often
help achieve a softer look, even
if the color is brighter. You will
benefit from your bridal party
wearing colors that do not clash
or contrast with your own look.

**ABOVE** *The Countess of Wessex
enhanced the soft white of her dress
with a stunning pearl necklace and
silk chiffon veil.*

### TIPS FOR THE DAY

- Your best look is to keep
highlighting your hair.
- Matte, textured jewelry and
pearls will look fantastic on you.

## ACCENT COLORS

| CLARET | SALMON PINK | ROSE PINK | CHARCOAL BLUE | VERBENA | JADE | LIGHT PERIWINKLE | AMETHYST |

# looking good in whites

WHITE IS TRADITIONALLY ASSOCIATED WITH BRIDAL GOWNS. IT COMES IN MANY DIFFERENT SHADES, AND YOU
NEED TO MAKE SURE THAT IF YOU GO FOR A REAL WHITE WEDDING DRESS YOU CHOOSE THE VERY BEST WHITE
FOR YOU. KNOWING YOUR DOMINANT COLORING WILL HELP YOU SELECT THE APPROPRIATE SHADE.

## which white should you wear?

**LIGHT** Your white is a translucent white such as gardenia, which has a gentle subtlety to it.
**Fabric** Select as sheer a fabric as you can take to balance with your scale: are you petite, average, or grand?

**DEEP** For your strong coloring you need a bold, intense white, such as chalk white.
**Fabric** The strength of the color will be enhanced by heavier fabrics.

**WARM** The choice of white for you needs a little thought. Balance the warm tones of your coloring with jasmine white, which contains a hint of yellow.
**Fabric** The use of texture, as in a shantung silk, will soften the clarity of the white.

**COOL** Pure white will look good against your coloring. If you are very pale, a slight natural tan will enhance the white.
**Fabric** Pure white lace gives you the option of softening the "hard" quality of this color.

**CLEAR** The stunning clarity of orchid white will provide you with a backdrop for a colorful and stunning bouquet.
**Fabric** Make sure that the fabric you choose shines.

**SOFT** Your soft white is the gentlest white of all. Its tone can often be achieved by selecting texture in the fabric.
**Fabric** Matte fabrics will absorb the light and therefore soften the color.

**LIGHT** *Your coloring is flattered by nearly every shade of white. One of the best for you is gardenia, which is softer than pure white. This will balance with your delicate coloring.*

**CLEAR** *With your contrasting coloring, your choice of white needs to be one that has clarity to it. Orchid white is the best choice for you; you then have the opportunity to use contrasting accessories to balance your look.*

## Deep

Chalk white is a deep, rich white and will look great in a textured fabric, which will intensify the color. Don't be afraid of some bold-colored flowers in your bouquet—they will offset wonderfully against your chalk-white dress.

## Cool

Your best white is a pure white that has absolutely no yellow tones in it whatsoever. If you think that this color might be a little harsh, think about having it in a soft satin or silk, or with an overlay of lace.

## Warm

The perfect beige for you is antique gold, which is available in many different fabrics, both shiny and matte. This is a stunning color for you to wear and is suitable for all types of wedding dress.

## Clear

Taupe is a bright shade of beige, so if you are looking for something different for your wedding dress you may choose to wear this, with some added details to complement your clear coloring and bright eyes.

# pastel greens

TRADITIONALLY, GREEN WAS NOT CONSIDERED A COLOR A BRIDE WOULD CHOOSE TO WEAR. HOWEVER, IN TODAY'S ENVIRONMENTALLY AWARE SOCIETY, GREEN HAS BECOME INCREASINGLY FASHIONABLE AND POPULAR IN WOMEN'S WEAR. PASTEL GREENS WILL GIVE YOUR WEDDING DRESS A MODERN AND INNOVATIVE LOOK.

**LIGHT**
APPLE WHITE

**DEEP**
GOOSEBERRY

**WARM**
YELLOW-GREEN

**COOL**
ICE GREEN

**CLEAR**
MINT

**SOFT**
WILLOW

**RIGHT** *Here our light bride wears a beautiful dress in apple white.*

# greens

THERE IS SOMETHING CREATIVE AND UNUSUAL ABOUT CHOOSING GREEN FOR YOUR WEDDING OUTFIT. YOUR CHOICE OF SHADE MIGHT BE AFFECTED BY THE TIME OF YEAR: A PINE-GREEN DRESS AT A CHRISTMAS WEDDING WILL SET THE SCENE, WHILE IN SPRING AN APPLE-GREEN GOWN CAN BE FUN AND DIFFERENT.

**LIGHT**
APPLE GREEN

**DEEP**
MOSS

**WARM**
LIME

**COOL**
BLUE-GREEN

**CLEAR**
EMERALD GREEN

**SOFT**
VERBENA

**RIGHT** *Our deep bride is wearing a vintage-style dress in light moss.*

# blues

YOU HAVE A CHOICE OF VARIOUS SHADES OF BLUE, DEPENDING ON YOUR DOMINANT COLORING. YOU CAN LIGHTEN OR DEEPEN YOUR SHADE BY USING THE BLUE AS A BASE FABRIC WITH A SHEER WHITE OR CREAM OVER THE TOP OR, ALTERNATIVELY, YOU COULD USE A BLUE GEORGETTE OR LACE OVER WHITE OR CREAM.

**LIGHT**

SKY BLUE

**DEEP**

TRUE BLUE

**WARM**

LAPIS

**COOL**

CORNFLOWER

**CLEAR**

CHINESE BLUE

**SOFT**

FORGET-ME-NOT

**RIGHT** *Our cool bride's cornflower dress complements her coloring.*

# aquas, teals, and light blues

IF YOUR WEDDING IS TAKING PLACE AT THE HEIGHT OF SUMMER OR IN A TROPICAL LOCATION, YOU MIGHT WANT TO CHOOSE A BEAUTIFUL AQUA OR TEAL, WHICH WILL GIVE A FEELING OF LIGHT AND FRESHNESS TO THE DAY. LIGHT BLUES ARE FLATTERING AGAINST MOST SKIN TYPES AND A GREAT ALTERNATIVE TO WHITE.

**LIGHT**
SEA GREEN

**DEEP**
TURQUOISE

**WARM**
AQUA

**COOL**
DUCK EGG

**CLEAR**
LIGHT TEAL

**SOFT**
EAU DE NIL

**RIGHT** *Eau de nil is a perfect choice for our soft bride.*

# pastel pinks

IF YOU HAVE A ROMANTIC AND FEMININE PERSONALITY, YOU MAY CHOOSE TO WEAR PINK ON YOUR WEDDING DAY. THE SHADE YOU CHOOSE FOR YOUR BLUSH AND LIPSTICK MUST BALANCE AND WORK IN HARMONY WITH YOUR CHOSEN PINK, PARTICULARLY IF YOU ARE WARM OR COOL.

**LIGHT**
PASTEL PINK

**DEEP**
BLUSH PINK

**WARM**
PEACH

**COOL**
ICY PINK

**CLEAR**
LIGHT APRICOT

**SOFT**
SHELL PINK

**RIGHT** *Icy pink balances perfectly with our cool bride.*

# reds

TO ADD DRAMA TO YOUR WEDDING DRESS, YOU MAY WANT TO GO FOR RED. IT CAN BE HEAD TO TOE, OR YOU MAY CHOOSE TO MAKE YOUR DRESS A TWO-PIECE WITH ONE PART RED. IN SOME SOCIETIES, RED IS THE TRADITIONAL WEDDING DRESS COLOR, SO MAKE SURE IT IS THE RIGHT RED FOR YOU.

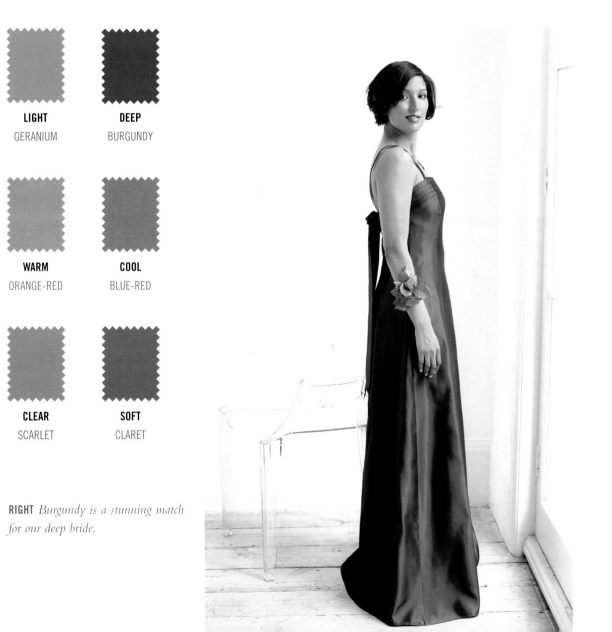

**LIGHT**
GERANIUM

**DEEP**
BURGUNDY

**WARM**
ORANGE-RED

**COOL**
BLUE-RED

**CLEAR**
SCARLET

**SOFT**
CLARET

**RIGHT** *Burgundy is a stunning match for our deep bride.*

# purples

THERE IS NOTHING MORE STUNNING THAN A PURPLE OR BLUE GOWN AT AN EVENING WEDDING. THE DARKER COLORS ARE VERY FLATTERING AND SLIMMING, WHILE THE SOFTER SHADES WILL HAVE A CALMING AND RELAXING EFFECT ON THE BRIDE AND HER PARTY.

**LIGHT**
VIOLET

**DEEP**
DAMSON

**WARM**
LIGHT PERIWINKLE

**COOL**
BRIGHT PERIWINKLE

**CLEAR**
PURPLE

**SOFT**
SOFT VIOLET

**RIGHT** *Our clear bride looks amazing in purple and cyclamen pink.*

# metallics and blacks

IF YOU REALLY WANT A WEDDING WITH A DIFFERENCE, THEN CHOOSING METALLICS AND/OR SHADES OF BLACK WILL GIVE YOU THE DESIRED EFFECT. ONLY THOSE WITH DEEP COLORING CAN WEAR BLACK FROM HEAD TO TOE; OTHER COLORING TYPES SHOULD ONLY USE IT AS A TRIM.

**LIGHT**
ICE GRAY

**DEEP**
BLACK

**WARM**
BRONZE

**COOL**
SILVER

**CLEAR**
CHARCOAL

**SOFT**
PEWTER

**RIGHT** *Our warm bride just glows in a bronze wedding dress.*

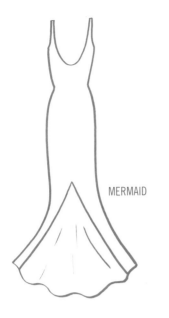

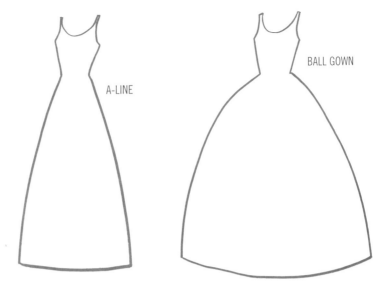

MERMAID

A-LINE

BALL GOWN

a good shape if you are small-busted. The skirt will flare out gently from where the waist seam finishes, and its fullness should be determined by your height: the taller you are, the fuller the skirt can be. This is a wonderful style to wear if you are going for comfort first, or in a flowing fabric if you are a mother-to-be.

## bias cut

The secret of the bias-cut dress lies in the cutting of the fabric. This is done across the grain of the cloth and gives a soft, fluid and feminine look to the finished dress, which will skim the hips gently. It is much more suitable for softer fabrics. If you want to incorporate a floating, fluid train, this is the ideal style to choose.

## mermaid

The mermaid is a variation of the sheath, with slightly more waist emphasis and a close-fitting skirt that fans out at the bottom, either all around or just at the back. This works best on a long style and is ideal for decorating all the way around. It creates a very glamorous look that will give the illusion of longer legs. However, be careful about where the skirt starts to flare—you need to be sure you can walk easily.

## A-line

This dress style is between the shift and the ball gown. The top is fitted and the skirt flares out as little or as much as you want. This style is ideally suited to a two-piece combination and is therefore the most flexible

for many brides—you can mix fabrics and colors. If you need to enhance your hips, pleats can be added to the skirt part of the dress as an extra detail.

## ball gown

This is the dress most brides dream about. The bodice is closely fitted and the skirt very full. It is extremely beautiful, with its layers upon layers of fabric, petticoats and train, often intricately decorated with beads, pearls, and sequins, but it is not always the most practical dress to wear—it is warm in the winter but not so good in the summer. If you are petite, keep the skirt volume to a minimum. This style works especially well if you have long legs or want to disguise full hips or thighs.

# fabrics

YOUR WEDDING DRESS IS ONE OF THE MOST EXPENSIVE DRESSES YOU WILL EVER BUY. THE FABRIC YOU SELECT WILL PLAY A KEY ROLE IN MAKING THAT DRESS FIT PERFECTLY, AND THIS IS THE MAKE-OR-BREAK OF THE PERFECT WEDDING DRESS. YOU WILL ALSO NEED TO CONSIDER WHAT EMBELLISHMENT, IF ANY, YOU WANT TO ADD TO THE FABRIC.

**ABOVE** *Lace and ribbons can both be used to add detail.*

## fabric factors

When you are looking at fabrics, there are three elements to consider:

**Weight** This is determined by the number of fibers spun into the thread of the yarn. The higher the number, the heavier the fabric. Lightweight fabrics have a fluid feel and will drape more easily.

**Texture** This is created by the weaving process and will give a smooth or raised finish. Some textures produce a matte finish, others shiny; some weaving processes, such as that used for damask, give a fabric matte and shine together.

**Fluidity** This depends on the type of yarn and the weaving process. Some fabrics, such as georgette, are loosely woven, which produces an easy draping characteristic. Tightly woven fabrics, like satin, drape less easily and feel crisp.

## selecting a fabric

The chart opposite provides a guide to the three elements of weight, texture, and fluidity for a range of fabrics and will help you make an informed choice. You may have your heart set on a luxury yarn such as silk, but do not automatically reject silk mixes—they are far less prone to creasing, and it may be easier to incorporate embellishments.

# lace

Most laces have their origins in earlier centuries in Europe. Lace is often used to enhance a plain-textured fabric or to add details to the dress. There are many different styles and weights of lace available, most originating from traditional and regional designs. When choosing lace, you will need to consider weight, texture, and the type of fabric it's being worn with.

**Alençon** Needlepoint lace with a raised motif on sheer net, outlined with heavier silk cording known as gimp.

**Chantilly** Delicate floral and ribboned design in heavy thread on a mesh background. Edges are scalloped.

**Guipure** Heavy, very textured lace with a raised design connected by threads.

**Ribbon** Not strictly a lace but ribbons sewn into patterns on various weights of net.

**Spanish** Flat lace, usually with a rose design.

**Venetian** Heavy lace with a raised, floral, or geometric design on an open background.

## EMBELLISHMENTS

Embellishments are added to a fabric to emphasize the style or to add details to a simple design. They can also enrich the fabric, giving it texture and individuality. Embellishments can be as simple as a few pearls or sequins added to the edge of a sleeve or as complex as an all-over pattern. Silk flowers and bows can add a touch of color that may link to your flowers and bridesmaids' or even the groom's outfits. Just make sure any embellishment does not draw attention to an area of your body you would rather not show off!

| FABRIC | WEIGHT* | TEXTURE | FLUIDITY |
|---|---|---|---|
| brocade | heavy | raised | crisp |
| chiffon | light | minimal | very fluid |
| damask | heavy | raised | crisp |
| duchess satin | variable | minimal | variable |
| dupioni | variable | slight | variable |
| georgette | light | minimal | fluid |
| moiré | variable | subtle | variable |
| organza | light | minimal | crisp |
| shantung silk | variable | slubbed | variable |
| silk crepe | variable | crinkled or grained | variable |
| taffeta | light | minimal | crisp |
| velvet | heavy | plush | medium |

*Some fabrics are available in various weights, which will affect their fluidity.
In these cases, the lighter the fabric, the more fluid it will be.

# your body shape

YOUR SIZE DOES NOT DETERMINE YOUR BODY SHAPE. WHATEVER SIZE YOU ARE, UNDERSTANDING YOUR BODY SHAPE WILL ENABLE YOU TO FINE-TUNE THE CHOICE OF DRESS STYLES THAT WILL COMPLEMENT YOU BEST. YOU MAY FIND YOU FALL BETWEEN TWO SHAPES, IN WHICH CASE YOU WILL NEED TO COMPARE WHICH DRESSES HAVE THE HIGHER STAR RATING IN BOTH SECTIONS (SEE PAGES 48–59). THE GREATER THE NUMBER OF STARS, THE BETTER THE DRESS STYLE IS FOR YOU.

## neat hourglass

Your bust is well defined and you have soft curves to your hips, bottom, and stomach. You generally have little difficulty in getting clothes to fit, so most styles will suit you as long as your proportions are balanced.

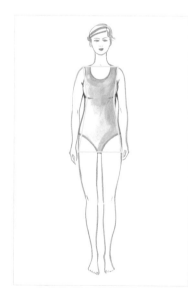

## full hourglass

You have a full bust, a well-defined waist, full hips, and possibly a curvy bottom. If you get a good fit on the hips you will often find the waist of skirts and pants is too large. Close-fitting designs are your best bet.

## triangle

Your bust may be minimal or full, and your shoulders probably narrow and sloping. You will have difficulty finding a sheath dress that fits properly. A dress with a full skirt will work well, as will separates.

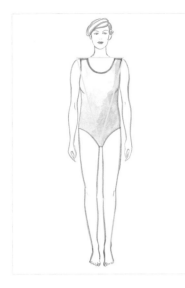

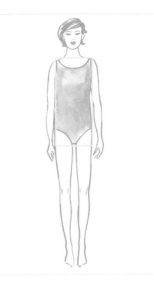

# inverted triangle

You may have a minimal or defined waist. Dresses that show off your shoulders are great for your shape. Straight-line styles work well on you, but avoid frills and flounces. You have the perfect shape to add details to your hips and bottom, if you wish.

# column

Your appearance is lean and long—you have a minimal bust, just a little shaping around your waist, and flat hips and bottom. You need to consider a dress that really enhances your body shape. A boned bodice and a fuller skirt will work well for you.

# rectangle

You may be full- or flat-chested, and your rib cage seems to go straight down to your waist. Your hips and bottom are flat, and you may carry a little weight around your middle. Straight styles are best for you, so look for a dress that gives the illusion of a waist.

## SCALE AND PROPORTIONS

When selecting a wedding dress, make sure that you take into account your scale (petite, average, grand) and proportions (high waisted, low waisted). These will affect the suitability of various designs.

• If you are petite, you should keep the details of your look small and delicate.

• If you have a larger-boned structure, you will be able to scale up the details and accessories.

• If you are low-waisted, a wedding dress style that gives the illusion of longer legs, such as empire line, will be perfect.

• If you are high-waisted, try a dress with a dropped waistline.

# neat hourglass

MOST DRESS STYLES WILL LOOK STUNNING ON YOU, SO YOU CAN TAKE YOUR PICK TO FIND YOUR DREAM DRESS. HOWEVER, YOU WILL NEED TO CONSIDER YOUR HEIGHT AND WHETHER YOU ARE HIGH- OR LOW-WAISTED.

★★★★★ EXCELLENT    ★★★★ VERY GOOD    ★★★ GOOD    ★★ NOT GREAT    ★ NOT FOR YOU

**BIAS CUT** ★★★★★ In soft fabric, this will drape over your figure beautifully and give you a floaty, ethereal look. This dress is best in a fluid and matte fabric.

**A-LINE** ★★★★★ This is the style that will flatter your balanced body shape and work well, whatever your height and proportions. For a straighter silhouette, choose a crisp fabric such as brocade. For a softer line, choose a silk crepe.

**MERMAID** ★★★★ This is a wonderful dress to show off your figure. It will give you a very feminine and curvy look. If you are not wearing a veil, there will still be interest at the back. Beware if you are petite, as the mermaid style can make you look shorter.

**EMPIRE** ★★★★ This style will help enhance a small bust. It will also give an illusion of longer legs. You can change the look of the dress by mixing different fabrics and textures for the top and bottom—say, lace on top and satin below.

**BALL GOWN** ★★★★ This is a real Cinderella dress if you are average to grand in height. Make sure that the volume of the skirt does not overpower your bone structure. In a crisp fabric, pleating will be better for the skirt; soft fabrics are better gathered.

**SHEATH** ★★★ This will be a comfortable dress to wear but it will not show off your figure. The softer the fabric, the more of your shape will show.

**RIGHT** *A bias-cut dress will hide nothing, so it is the perfect choice for a neat hourglass.*

# full hourglass

YOUR VOLUPTUOUS FEMININE FIGURE WILL BENEFIT FROM A CLOSE-FITTING DRESS IN SOFT FABRIC. THIS IS A FABULOUS OPPORTUNITY TO SHOW OFF YOUR TINY WAIST, FULL BUST, AND CURVY HIPS.

★★★★★ EXCELLENT ★★★★ VERY GOOD ★★★ GOOD ★★ NOT GREAT ★ NOT FOR YOU

**BALL GOWN** ★★★★★ The ball gown will emphasize your small waist, and if you want to disguise your hips and bottom this dress is for you. The skirt fabric should be held in soft gathers rather than pleats.

**MERMAID** ★★★★★ Your mermaid dress needs to be created in a soft silk or satin. Beware of gathers over the hips, which will add volume. You will need to balance the depth of the flare with your height and leg length.

**BIAS CUT** ★★★★ This dress is ideal for the average to petite bride. Careful choice of fabric is essential, since it needs to drape over your curves—soft silk crepe is ideal.

**A-LINE** ★★★★ This shape is good for you when worn as separates. The bodice can be boned to enhance your full bust and the skirt softly flared over your curved hips and bottom.

**EMPIRE** ★★ The empire shape will accentuate your full bust and should be enhanced with a wide cummerbund just below the waist to show off your lovely curvy figure.

**SHEATH** ★ A sheath will work best for you if you add some form of waist definition, such as a half-belt tied at the back, a narrow full belt, or a waisted jacket worn over the top. Make sure the fabric of the dress is soft.

**RIGHT** *A ball gown dress is what dreams are made of, and it is perfect for you.*

# triangle

TO GIVE THE ILLUSION OF A BALANCED FIGURE, YOU NEED TO BRING ATTENTION AND DETAILS TO THE TOP HALF OF YOUR BODY. THIS CAN BE DONE WITH FABRICS, LAYERING, AND EMBELLISHMENTS.

★★★★★ EXCELLENT   ★★★★ VERY GOOD   ★★★ GOOD   ★★ NOT GREAT   ★ NOT FOR YOU

**EMPIRE** ★★★★★ The empire-style dress lends itself to the addition of all kinds of details to the top half. Because of the loose-fitting skirt, your hips become invisible.

**A-LINE** ★★★★★ Have fun with the top half of your dress with a bolero, lace, or embroidery.  Keep the skirt volume down and pleating at the front or back of the skirt.

**BALL GOWN** ★★★★ Your fairy-tale dress needs a wide shoulder line to counterbalance the full skirt. Keep the fabric of the skirt simple and fluid.

**MERMAID** ★★ The mermaid dress will not hug your hips. It should look great on you if the detail is actually in the flare, which should start at knee level, thereby balancing the hips.

**BIAS CUT** ★ This figure-hugging dress needs some interest added to the top and layering in order to work for you. This could be in the form of a sheer coat or jacket that will float gently over your hips. Shoulder details will draw attention to the top half.

**SHEATH** ★ To enable this style to fit properly, make it a two-piece. If you alter the top of a sheath to fit you, the balance will change and it will not hang properly.

**RIGHT** *An empire wedding dress style will flatter you as well as giving ease of movement.*

# inverted triangle

YOU HAVE FANTASTIC SHOULDERS AND NARROW HIPS. THIS GIVES YOU THE OPPORTUNITY TO BRING ATTENTION TO THE LOWER HALF OF YOUR GOWN WHILE SHOWING OFF YOUR BEAUTIFUL SHOULDERS. YOU WILL FIND THAT CRISPER FABRICS WORK WELL OVER THE STRAIGHT LINES OF YOUR BODY, GIVING YOU AN UNCLUTTERED LOOK.

★★★★★ EXCELLENT   ★★★★ VERY GOOD   ★★★ GOOD   ★★ NOT GREAT   ★ NOT FOR YOU

**MERMAID** ★★★★★ A strapless style in crisp fabric with gentle gathering over the hips, flaring out at the bottom, will give you an amazing shape.

**SHEATH** ★★★★★ In a crisp fabric, this slightly waisted dress will follow the straight lines of your body. Think about adding peplums or exaggerated pleats over the hips for added interest and to balance your shoulder line.

**EMPIRE** ★★★★ Your choice of empire-style dress should always be in crisp fabric, hanging straight from underneath the bust—no gathers for you. If you have a cummerbund, it should be pleated rather than gathered.

**A-LINE** ★★★★ Make sure your skirt is flat-fronted, with pleats at the side to balance your silhouette. A close-fitting top with minimal embellishment will work well.

**BALL GOWN** ★★ If you are set on this dress style, again keep the fabric as crisp as possible and avoid gathers and rounded details. The top needs to be straight and fitted with an angled neckline.

**BIAS CUT** ★ This dress will not hang properly on your figure. However, if this is your dream look, layer it with Venetian lace in geometric designs and patterns.

**RIGHT** *A mermaid dress will emphasize your figure and create interest below the knees.*

# column

YOUR SVELTE FIGURE WILL BE ENHANCED BY USING TEXTURE AND INTERESTING DESIGN FEATURES ON YOUR

DRESS. IF YOU ARE ALSO PETITE, MAKE SURE THE WEIGHT OF THE FABRIC DOES NOT OVERWHELM YOUR FINE

BONE STRUCTURE.

★★★★★ EXCELLENT   ★★★★ VERY GOOD   ★★★ GOOD   ★★ NOT GREAT   ★ NOT FOR YOU

**A-LINE** ★★★★★ This dress can be made to enhance your upper body with a boned bodice to give you a fuller bust, which in turn will define your waist. The A-line of the skirt can be achieved with crisp fabrics or flat pleats.

**SHEATH** ★★★★ The simple style of this dress will benefit from embellishment, particularly in the bust and hip areas. If you are petite, this style will add height; if you are tall, consider a wide train.

**EMPIRE** ★★★★ By using textured or patterned fabrics such as brocade or lace, this dress shape will enhance your bust area. A soft, gathered skirt will give you a floaty, feminine look.

**MERMAID** ★★★ You have the perfect body for an Edwardian-style mermaid dress, with a lacy top and a bustle skirt to create detail over your hips and bottom.

**BALL GOWN** ★★ For your ball gown to work, it will need details above the waist such as sleeves and/or an interesting neckline. If you are at all bony, a beautiful lace covering over the bodice up to the neck will look very elegant.

**BIAS CUT** ★ The simple elegance of this shape will need to be enhanced by all-over embellishment or layering of the fabric.

**RIGHT** *A simple A-line dress will be elegant, and all the focus will be on you.*

# rectangle

CHOOSING THE RIGHT FABRIC WILL GUARANTEE THAT YOUR DRESS STYLE COMPLEMENTS YOUR BODY SHAPE. AVOID FINE, CLINGING FABRICS UNLESS YOU USE THEM LAYERED. YOUR BEST CHOICE IS A CRISPER, HEAVIER SATIN OR BROCADE. THE SILHOUETTE OF THE DRESS SHOULD BE KEPT SIMPLE AND MADE SPECIAL BY ADDING EMBELLISHMENTS AND DETAILS.

★★★★★ EXCELLENT     ★★★★ VERY GOOD     ★★★ GOOD     ★★ NOT GREAT     ★ NOT FOR YOU

**SHEATH** ★★★★★ The straight lines of the sheath will follow your body shape and make sure you are comfortable all day long. Details such as sleeves, an interesting neckline, and a train can make this simple dress the most glamorous one for you.

## MOTHER-TO-BE

If you are expecting a baby and have lost your waistline, you will temporarily be a fuller-shaped rectangle. In this case, the best dresses for you are the empire and sheath styles in soft fabrics only.

**EMPIRE** ★★★★ For a more feminine touch, an empire-style wedding dress will enable you to use slightly softer fabrics in the skirt. The seaming under the bust should be kept narrow. Feel free to add details to the back of the dress.

**MERMAID** ★★★ Your style of mermaid dress should skim gently over your body with details on the bust and hips. It can be fairly tight-fitting on your legs—make sure you have a split in it to enable you to walk.

**A-LINE** ★★★ The A-line will work for you if the bodice has a dropped waistline. The skirt should lie flat and flare out gently.

**BIAS CUT** ★★ The secret of making this dress work for you is to have it in a heavy, matte duchess satin or dupioni silk. This will make the dress hang straight and enhance your figure.

**BALL GOWN** ★ If this is your chosen dress, it needs to be as simple as possible, with the least amount of gathering at the waist. A dropped V-shape bodice will keep the skirt flat over your stomach.

**RIGHT** *A sheath will look striking with embellishment and details, such as petal sleeves.*

# details: bodices and waistlines

THE BODICE IS THE TOP PART OF THE GOWN AND IS OFTEN WHAT MAKES OR BREAKS THE DRESS FOR YOU.

YOU WILL NEED TO CONSIDER THE SHAPE OF THE NECKLINE (SEE PAGES 62–63) AND HOW FITTED THE BODICE

SHOULD BE, PARTICULARLY IF YOU HAVE SELECTED AN EMPIRE, A-LINE, MERMAID, OR BALL GOWN.

## beautiful bodices

The bodice can be simply shaped with seams or darts, as in a bias-cut or shift dress, or elaborate, with boning, as in a corset type. Often the bodice will be embellished (see page 45). The back is as important as the front and may be one of the most intricate parts of the dress. The bodice must fit perfectly and might need to be refitted at the last minute if you have lost weight, as often the whole structure of the dress hangs from it. If you have an average-sized bust, you can try all the different types of bodice.

## perfect waistlines

The shape of the bodice also includes the waistline, which can be positioned at various points depending on proportions.

**RIGHT** *Remember that many people will see you from the back!*

**BONED**

FULL BUST • SMALL BUST

**OVERLAY**

SMALL BUST

**GATHERING**

SMALL BUST

**PLEATING**

SMALL BUST

**BACKLESS**

SMALL BUST

**CORSETED BACK**

FULL BUST • SMALL BUST

**LACING AT BACK**

FULL BUST • SMALL BUST

**BACK STRAPS**

FULL BUST • SMALL BUST

**INSERT**

SMALL BUST

**STRAPLESS**

SMALL BUST

**EMPIRE**

LOW WAIST • NO WAIST

**NATURAL**

LOW WAIST • HIGH WAIST

**ASYMMETRIC**

HIGH WAIST • NO WAIST

**V-SHAPED BASQUE**

HIGH WAIST

**DROPPED**

HIGH WAIST • NO WAIST

# details: necklines

WHATEVER THE STYLE OF YOUR DRESS, YOU NEED TO THINK ABOUT THE BEST NECKLINES FOR YOU. YOU WILL NEED TO CONSIDER THE LENGTH OF YOUR NECK, ITS WIDTH, YOUR UPPER CHEST, AND HOW COMFORTABLE YOU ARE WITH SHOWING SOME FLESH AND CLEAVAGE.

### EDWARDIAN/MANDARIN
LONG NECK • THIN NECK
• SMALL BUST

### SCOOP
LONG NECK • WIDE NECK •
WIDE, STRAIGHT SHOULDERS
• NARROW, SLOPING SHOULDERS
• FULL BUST • SMALL BUST

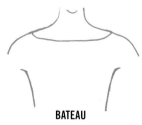

### BATEAU
THIN NECK • FULL BUST • SMALL BUST

### STAND-UP
LONG NECK • WIDE NECK • THICK NECK
• WIDE, STRAIGHT SHOULDERS •
NARROW, SLOPING SHOULDERS
• FULL BUST • SMALL BUST

### SPAGHETTI
SHORT NECK • WIDE NECK •
WIDE, STRAIGHT SHOULDERS

**RIGHT** *A sweetheart neckline is enhanced with details below the bust.*

### V-SHAPED
SHORT NECK • WIDE NECK
• WIDE, STRAIGHT SHOULDERS
• NARROW, SLOPING SHOULDERS
• FULL BUST

**COWL**

SHORT NECK • WIDE NECK • THIN NECK

• NARROW, SLOPING SHOULDERS

• FULL BUST • SMALL BUST

**HALTER**

WIDE, STRAIGHT SHOULDERS

**TANK**

SHORT NECK • WIDE NECK

• WIDE, STRAIGHT SHOULDERS

**ASYMMETRIC**

LONG NECK • THICK NECK •

WIDE, STRAIGHT SHOULDERS

• SMALL BUST

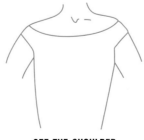

**OFF-THE-SHOULDER**

LONG NECK • SHORT NECK • WIDE

NECK • THICK NECK • FULL BUST

• SMALL BUST

**SWEETHEART**

LONG NECK • SHORT NECK •

WIDE NECK • THIN NECK

• WIDE, STRAIGHT SHOULDERS •

NARROW, SLOPING SHOULDERS

• FULL BUST • SMALL BUST

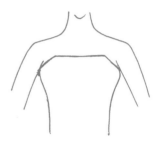

**STRAIGHT STRAPLESS**

LONG NECK • SHORT NECK

• WIDE NECK • THICK NECK

• WIDE, STRAIGHT SHOULDERS

• SMALL BUST

**JEWEL**

LONG NECK • THIN NECK

• WIDE, STRAIGHT SHOULDERS

• NARROW, SLOPING SHOULDERS •

FULL BUST • SMALL BUST

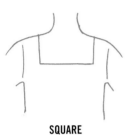

**SQUARE**

SHORT NECK •

WIDE, STRAIGHT SHOULDERS

• NARROW, SLOPING SHOULDERS

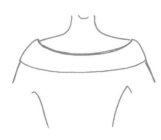

**BARDOT**

LONG NECK • SHORT NECK • THIN NECK

• NARROW, SLOPING SHOULDERS •

FULL BUST • SMALL BUST.

# details: sleeves

FASHION OR THE TIME OF THE YEAR DICTATE THAT MOST STYLES OF WEDDING GOWN COME WITHOUT SLEEVES. HOWEVER, THIS MAY NOT ALWAYS BE SUITABLE, AND YOU SHOULD CONSIDER A RANGE OF FACTORS THAT MAY MEAN YOU WOULD PREFER A DRESS WITH SLEEVES.

**ABOVE** *Not everyone has perfect arms; or you might have a winter wedding. Here a beautiful lace shrug is the perfect solution.*

## sleeves or sleeveless

Think about the following when making a decision as to whether or not your dress should be sleeveless:

• Type of ceremony; you may want your arms covered.

• General condition of your arms.

• Length of your arms.

• Size of your bust.

• Fullness, or otherwise, of your upper arms.

If sleeves are simply not available for your chosen style of dress, consider a cover-up in the form of a bolero, jacket, coat, or cape (see page 88).

## making a choice

There are many types of sleeves suitable for either a dress or a cover-up. The fabric you choose for your sleeves doesn't necessarily have to be the same as that for the main body of the dress. You may want to consider lace, chiffon and other see-through fabrics to give the illusion of a sleeve but without the weight.

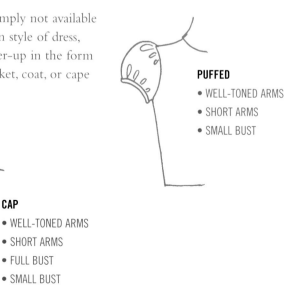

**PUFFED**
• WELL-TONED ARMS
• SHORT ARMS
• SMALL BUST

**CAP**
• WELL-TONED ARMS
• SHORT ARMS
• FULL BUST
• SMALL BUST

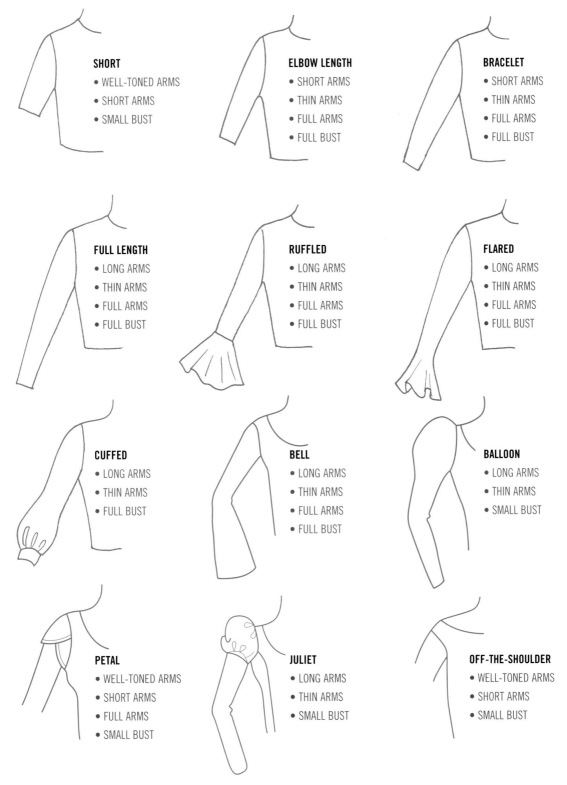

**SHORT**
- WELL-TONED ARMS
- SHORT ARMS
- SMALL BUST

**ELBOW LENGTH**
- SHORT ARMS
- THIN ARMS
- FULL ARMS
- FULL BUST

**BRACELET**
- SHORT ARMS
- THIN ARMS
- FULL ARMS
- FULL BUST

**FULL LENGTH**
- LONG ARMS
- THIN ARMS
- FULL ARMS
- FULL BUST

**RUFFLED**
- LONG ARMS
- THIN ARMS
- FULL ARMS
- FULL BUST

**FLARED**
- LONG ARMS
- THIN ARMS
- FULL ARMS
- FULL BUST

**CUFFED**
- LONG ARMS
- THIN ARMS
- FULL BUST

**BELL**
- LONG ARMS
- THIN ARMS
- FULL ARMS
- FULL BUST

**BALLOON**
- LONG ARMS
- THIN ARMS
- SMALL BUST

**PETAL**
- WELL-TONED ARMS
- SHORT ARMS
- FULL ARMS
- SMALL BUST

**JULIET**
- LONG ARMS
- THIN ARMS
- SMALL BUST

**OFF-THE-SHOULDER**
- WELL-TONED ARMS
- SHORT ARMS
- SMALL BUST

# details: trains

## making a choice

The overriding factors in your choice are the shape of your dress and the practicalities of it all. The train will give added weight to your dress, and you may even want to consider having it made to be detached when appropriate. An alternative is a train made in a lightweight fabric that will give a more fluid and floaty feel.

## PRACTICALITIES

Don't forget that if your train is permanently attached to your dress you will need to think of how you walk, sit, and dance with it. There are various ways to help you hold it. These include a loop you can attach to your wrist, a tape that enables you to gather up the train, or cleverly positioned hooks and eyes.

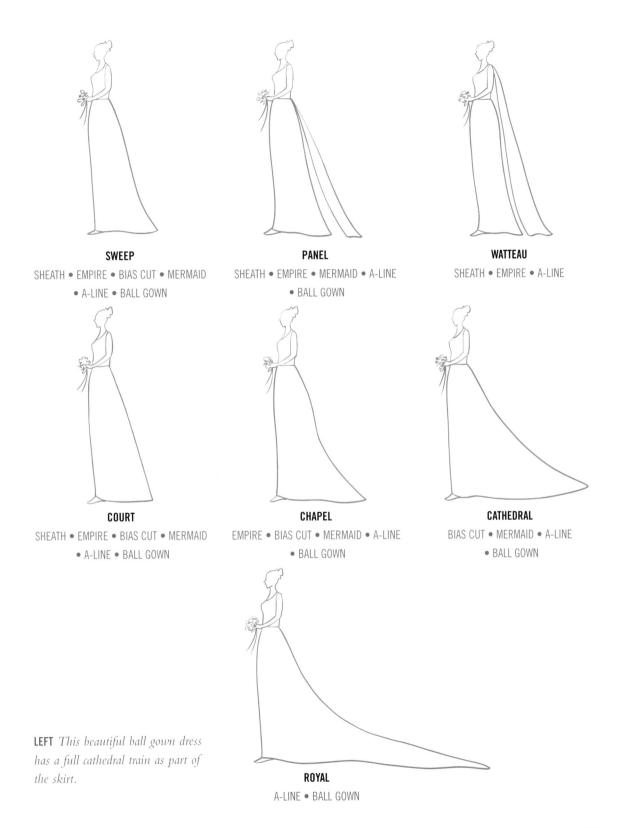

**SWEEP**

SHEATH • EMPIRE • BIAS CUT • MERMAID
• A-LINE • BALL GOWN

**PANEL**

SHEATH • EMPIRE • MERMAID • A-LINE
• BALL GOWN

**WATTEAU**

SHEATH • EMPIRE • A-LINE

**COURT**

SHEATH • EMPIRE • BIAS CUT • MERMAID
• A-LINE • BALL GOWN

**CHAPEL**

EMPIRE • BIAS CUT • MERMAID • A-LINE
• BALL GOWN

**CATHEDRAL**

BIAS CUT • MERMAID • A-LINE
• BALL GOWN

**LEFT** *This beautiful ball gown dress has a full cathedral train as part of the skirt.*

**ROYAL**

A-LINE • BALL GOWN

# alternative outfits

YOU MAY DECIDE THAT A FORMAL BRIDAL GOWN IS NOT WHAT YOU WANT TO WEAR AT YOUR WEDDING, OR YOU MAY HAVE DONE THE FORMAL BRIDAL GOWN BEFORE. THERE ARE MANY ELEGANT ALTERNATIVES WHERE YOUR BEST COLORS AND STYLES CAN COME INTO THEIR OWN.

## making a choice

There are several alternative outfits from which to choose:
• Three-piece outfit.
• Evening/cocktail dress.
• Dress and coat.
• Pantsuit.
Aspects you need to consider when choosing what to wear include your personality, the style of the occasion, the likely weather, the venue, and what you feel comfortable wearing.

The rules of dressing your body are the same, no matter what you decide to wear.

## jackets and coats

**Neat hourglass** Most styles will suit you, as long as you choose the right length. If you are petite, a short coat and dress combination will make you appear taller; alternatively, a short jacket and long skirt will achieve the same objective. Also make sure the sleeves stop at the break of your wrist. If you are grand scale, some definition (belt, pockets, lapels) using a contrasting color or other details will break the length and take the attention where you want it.

**Full hourglass** Focus on fabrics that have a draping quality. Avoid sharp lapels—a soft collar or collarless jacket or coat will work well. Also avoid details (including pockets) over the bust and hips. A jacket with a peplum (a flared ruffle coming from the waist) will look good.

**Triangle** Consider choosing a patterned jacket or coat over a plain dress or skirt to bring attention to the top half of your body. Interesting embellishments on the jacket can also help achieve this.

**Inverted triangle** A constructed jacket with crisp, sharp lines and straight darts will skim your silhouette. Make sure

the jacket finishes at hip level to balance with your shoulders.

**Column** A slightly waisted jacket or coat with details in the bust and hip areas will give the illusion of a shapely body. Avoid very soft, floaty fabrics.

**Rectangle** A jacket or coat with some shaping at the waist will work for you. The fuller your shape, the softer the fabric should be. Avoid details on the jacket such as full belts and frills.

# skirts

**Neat hourglass** To make sure that your skirt fits properly, you will need a waistband and some darting. Skirts should finish at a point where your leg is narrow—above the knee, on the knee, or at the lower calf.

**Full hourglass** Try a skirt that has some shaping, such as bias cut, flip, or paneled. A straight skirt will ride up and may look too small for you.

**Triangle** Make sure that your skirt does not curve under or grab your fullest part—it needs to hang straight from that point. Avoid too much volume.

**Inverted triangle** You can choose a skirt with straight-line details such as pleating, paneling, or stitching. A skirt with some kick at the bottom will help balance your shoulders.

**Column** Consider an A-line skirt that has a slight flare to it. Details and patterns on the skirt will also be good for you.

**Rectangle** Choose a skirt with no waistband or a dropped waist. Straight styles are good, and if the skirt is long a slit will provide a little glamour.

**RIGHT** *A stylish and detailed suit makes a great alternative to a classic wedding dress.*

# dresses

**Neat hourglass** With your balanced body line, the choice is yours. You may need to take your proportions into consideration to achieve a balanced look.

**Full hourglass** Choose a dress style that is soft and fluid. The ideal is a wrap or bias-cut dress that will drape.

**Triangle** A dress is not a good choice for you, because finding the right fit will be difficult. Consider separates instead.

**Inverted triangle** A sheath in a crisp fabric will be a good choice for you. The lines of the dress need some structure, and hip details (such as pockets) will work well.

**Column** Choose a dress that has slight waist emphasis, such as a half belt at the back.

**Rectangle** Make the most of your straight lines by wearing a simple sheath in a luxurious fabric. Details should be kept simple to keep your silhouette straight and uncluttered.

**BELOW** *The 1920s flapper dress is great for a woman without too many curves.*

## VINTAGE DRESSES

You may be lucky enough to have the opportunity of wearing a family dress, or be able to buy a vintage outfit that will be unique to you. If you are eager to recycle a dress already worn or to acquire one from an antique or secondhand store, you may need to have it altered to fit—half a century or so ago, women were generally much smaller. Alternatively, you can incorporate pieces of the vintage dress into a new one: lace and other embellishments can be transferred by a dressmaker or tailor.

completing the look

# your face shape

ON YOUR WEDDING DAY, YOU WILL BE PHOTOGRAPHED FROM EVERY ANGLE BY YOUR OFFICIAL PHOTOGRAPHER

AND MANY OTHERS, AND YOU WILL WANT TO BE CERTAIN THAT ALL ANGLES ARE YOUR BEST!

## a perfect picture

To look beautiful from all aspects, you will need to make sure that your hair, veil, headdress, and jewelry all work well with your face shape. You need to plan for the way your hair is styled, where you place your headpiece, and how the veil is attached and falls, in order for all these elements to work together to achieve a well-balanced look and the perfect head shot. Remember to take your headpiece and veil with you to the hairdresser when you go for a practice run.

**LEFT** *An oval face shape can wear any style headpiece and veil.*

## oval

You have balanced features and slightly rounded cheeks that narrow down to the jawline. Your chin may be slightly pointed or rounded, and your forehead is narrower than your cheekbones.

## square

Your whole face looks angled. The width and length are basically equal. Your jawline is straight and in line with your cheekbones, and your forehead is fairly square.

**ABOVE** *A square-shaped face is flattered by having a fuller hairstyle at the temples.*

## rectangle

Your face appears narrow, with the length greater than the width. Your forehead is high but square, and your jawline is angled. Your cheekbones may be pronounced.

## inverted triangle

You have a wide forehead, and your jawline is much narrower than your cheekbones. Your chin appears a little pointed.

## round

Your face is narrower at the forehead, fuller at the cheekbones and rounded down to the jawline. Your cheeks are full, and your whole face has a soft appearance.

# oval

YOUR OVAL FACE SHAPE IS PERFECTLY BALANCED. THE ONLY CONSIDERATION TO TAKE INTO ACCOUNT IS WHETHER YOU HAVE ANY FACIAL FEATURES THAT ARE NOT IN PROPORTION (SEE PAGES 86–87). HEADPIECES AND JEWELRY ARE DESCRIBED IN DETAIL ON PAGES 83–85, MAKEUP ON PAGES 119–124.

## LONG HAIR UP

Look at the back of your head to see if it is nicely curved, in which case any style will do. If it is flat, a hairstyle with volume at the back will balance the shape.

## LONG HAIR DOWN

Have your hair as natural or styled as you wish.

## SHORT HAIR

To show off your face, avoid having too much hair coming forward on to your forehead.

## HEADPIECE

A soft-line headpiece is better for you than an angled style.

## JEWELRY

Your guidelines for size will depend on whether you are petite, average, or grand in scale. Balance the dimensions of your jewelry to match.

## MAKEUP

Gently slant your eyebrows upward at the end. Apply a hint of blush around your temples and on the tip of your chin.

# square

YOUR SQUARE-SHAPED FACE WILL BE ENHANCED BY ADDING SOFT CONTOURS WITH YOUR HAIRSTYLE AND MAKEUP APPLICATION. WHICHEVER WAY YOU DECIDE TO WEAR YOUR HAIR, TRY TO ACHIEVE SOME FULLNESS AT THE SIDES TO GIVE THE ILLUSION OF A MORE OVAL-SHAPED FACE.

### LONG HAIR UP

If you are putting your hair up, you will need to add width to the sides of your temples. Either backcomb your hair here before pulling it back, or keep some hair loose around the temples to achieve this balance.

### LONG HAIR DOWN

Try a layered cut with feathering onto your face, which will soften its outline.

### SHORT HAIR

A rounded, layered cut with volume on the sides of the temples will be perfect for you. Avoid a one-length bob finishing at the jawline, with straight bangs.

### HEADPIECE

Crown, tiara, or wreath styles will soften the sharp angles of your face.

### JEWELRY

Avoid geometric styles: instead, select softer, rounder shapes.

### MAKEUP

Apply darker shading on your jawline and keep the line of your blush curved.

# rectangle

WITH THIS SHAPE, THE OVERALL IDEA IS TO CREATE THE ILLUSION THAT YOU HAVE A SHORTER FACE. THIS MAY BE ACHIEVED IN MANY DIFFERENT WAYS, BUT SOME SORT OF BANGS OVER THE FOREHEAD WILL ALWAYS HELP. IF YOU HAVE A LONG NECK CONSIDER A CHOKER-STYLE NECKLACE OR A DRESS WITH SOME FORM OF COLLAR.

### LONG HAIR UP

Bangs will be perfect for you. Wear the bulk of your hair at the nape of your neck rather than on the top, which would elongate your face even more.

### LONG HAIR DOWN

Keep your bangs and have your hair layered to soften your face. Avoid a center part.

### SHORT HAIR

Choose a layered style, flicked out to add width to your face.

### HEADPIECE

A Juliet cap will keep the length of your face to a minimum; alternatively, a narrow tiara would also be good. A fascinator slanted on the side will add width to your face.

### JEWELRY

Your earrings will need to add width to your face, so avoid long, dangling styles. Also avoid long chain necklaces.

### MAKEUP

Bring your eye shadow outward and upward to give width to your face. Define your blush closer to the hair and outer cheekbones.

# inverted triangle

BY ADDING VOLUME AND INTEREST TO YOUR JAWLINE YOU CAN GIVE THE ILLUSION OF A NARROWER FOREHEAD AND CHEEKBONES. THINK CAREFULLY ABOUT THE CHOICE OF NECKLINE ON YOUR WEDDING DRESS. A DEEP V WILL ONLY EMPHASIZE YOUR NARROW CHIN. A SCOOP OR ROUNDED NECKLINE WILL BE MORE FLATTERING.

### LONG HAIR UP
You need soft curls to fall from all around the hairline of a swept-up style.

### LONG HAIR DOWN
A flicked-out, layered style will add width around your jawline.

### SHORT HAIR
Feathered, rounded bangs will soften your forehead. You'll need volume at the jawline—your hair can be flicked under or out.

### HEADPIECE
Choose a headpiece style that can be worn at the back of your head, or try individual pins or small combs.

### JEWELRY
Dangling earrings with interest at the bottom are perfect for you. If you choose to wear studs, balance them with an interesting necklace if your dress can take it.

### MAKEUP
Make your lips the focal point of your face, using a lipgloss over your lipstick. Apply blush to the apples of your cheeks.

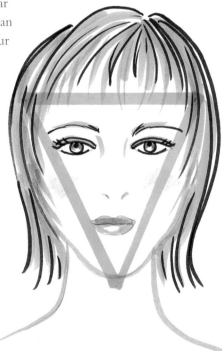

# round

YOUR ROUND, FEMININE FACE IS THE PERFECT CANVAS FOR SLIGHTLY MORE ANGLED HAIRSTYLES AND MAKEUP APPLICATIONS. ALTHOUGH YOU MAY WANT TO HAVE YOUR LONG HAIR PULLED UP, THIS WILL ONLY MAKE YOUR FACE LOOK ROUNDER, SO TRY A STYLE WHERE SOME OF YOUR HAIR FALLS ONTO YOUR FACE.

**LONG HAIR UP**

A French twist will give a slightly elongated look to your head, ensuring that you have some volume at the top.

**LONG HAIR DOWN**

An asymmetrical part and bangs work especially well if you are wearing your hair down and loose.

**SHORT HAIR**

A feathered style coming forward onto your face will suit you best.

**HEADPIECE**

A slightly taller or angled tiara or headpiece will be perfect.

**JEWELRY**

Neat-fitting earrings are best for you—avoid hoops.

**MAKEUP**

Keep your eyebrows as straight as possible. Use a highlighter straight along your cheekbones to create some contour.

# jewelry

FOR YOUR WEDDING, JEWELRY SHOULD BE KEPT TO A MINIMUM SO THAT IT IS YOU WHO SHINES ON THE DAY. YOUR CHOICE OF JEWELRY WILL DEPEND ON THE STYLE OF YOUR DRESS AND YOUR PROPORTIONS. YOU MAY EVEN DECIDE TO WEAR A FABULOUS FAMILY HEIRLOOM.

**ABOVE** *Keep your jewelry simple to avoid detracting from your wedding dress.*

**RIGHT** *You may choose to wear a matching comb in your hair.*

## earrings

• Small or stud-style earrings will suit all. These can be diamonds, pearls, or any other gemstones.

• Drop or dangling earrings are best worn with your hair away from your face—really long ones require a long neck.

## necklaces

Necklaces should be chosen with the neckline of your dress in mind: the lower the neckline, the more detailed your necklace can be.

• If your bodice is heavily embellished, a simple necklace is best, or none at all.

• A choker requires a long neck and low neckline.

## bracelets and watches

• If your dress has long sleeves, do not clutter your wrists with bracelets and a watch.

• If you want to wear a watch, choose one that is jeweled.

## rings

• Wear only your engagement ring, but not on your ring finger. Transfer it to the third finger of your right hand, so that your ring finger is free to receive your wedding ring. You can slip your engagement ring back on after the ceremony.

# headpieces and veils

A HEADPIECE AND VEIL WILL COMPLETE YOUR OVERALL LOOK. CHOOSING THE RIGHT ONES FOR YOU DEPENDS ON YOUR PERSONAL STYLE AND PREFERENCES, AS WELL AS THE DRESS YOU WILL BE WEARING. YOU'LL ALSO NEED TO THINK ABOUT THE HAIRSTYLE YOU WANT ON THE DAY, TO ENSURE THAT EVERYTHING WORKS IN HARMONY.

**ABOVE** *This cathedral spotted net veil is trimmed with scalloped edge lace for a romantic look.*

## headpieces

**Tiara** Jeweled or beaded semicircle of various heights, worn on top of the head toward the front. A tiara will give height to your face or forehead and can be rounded or angled, depending on the shape of your face. A rounded shape will soften an angled face (square or rectangle), while an angular tiara will give contours to a round face.

**Crown** Jeweled or beaded full circle of various heights, worn on top of the head. A crown will add height to any face, so avoid it if you have a rectangle face shape.

**Alice band** Band of various widths that fits closely to the head and is tucked behind the ears. It can be jeweled, beaded, or covered in the same fabric as used for your dress. An Alice band is good for all face shapes except inverted triangle.

TIARA

CROWN

ALICE BAND

SNOOD

BUN WRAP

JULIET CAP

WREATH

COMB

HAIRPINS

FASCINATOR

**Snood** Decorated net that encases your hair at the back of your head. A snood sits low on the back of the head, so avoid it if you have a short neck.

**Bun wrap** Decoration with which to wrap you hair if you are wearing it up in a bun. The wrap can be decorated with beads or sequins to coordinate with your dress. Worn on the back of the head, it is particularly good if the back of your head is flat.

**Juliet cap** Small, circular, decorated cap that fits on top of your head, to which a train can be attached. It works best with a long neck.

**Wreath** Crownlike garland made of fresh or silk flowers that rests on the head. A wreath is particularly good if you have a high forehead or rectangular face. It is best avoided if you have a low forehead or an especially round face.

**Comb** Available in various sizes and depths either to decorate or to keep your hair and veil in place. Because the long teeth grip well, a comb will keep a section of hair secure. It can be embellished with flowers or beads.

**Hairpins** Single pieces of decoration to be scattered throughout the hairstyle for a relaxed look.

**Fascinator** Small cap decorated with all sizes of feathers, ribbons, and flowers, worn slightly on the side of the head. Make sure you have enough hair for the fascinator to sit firmly and securely in it—elastic bands at the back of your hair is not a good look!

## veils

The volume and the length of your veil will depend on your height and the line of your dress. Also take into account how formal your wedding is. Traditionally some ceremonies call for the bride to wear a veil, which is often removed for the celebrations afterward.

**Flyaway** Informal veil that reaches to the shoulders and can be multilayered.

**Elbow** Veil that reaches to the elbow.

**Fingertip** Veil that falls to the tip of the fingers.

**Double tier** Two-layered veil in which the shorter layer is worn over the face during the first part of the ceremony, if desired. The second layer, which can be of any length, remains at the back.

**Chapel** Veil that reaches the bottom of the dress.

**Cathedral** Longest and most dramatic of all veils, falling to the floor behind the dress.

FLYAWAY          ELBOW

FINGERTIP          DOUBLE TIER

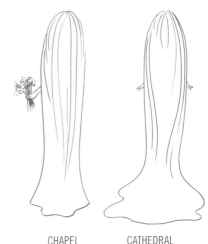

CHAPEL          CATHEDRAL

# disguise and hide: questions and answers

SOMETIMES THERE MAY BE ASPECTS OF YOUR FACE OR BODY YOU ARE UNHAPPY ABOUT. WITH THE CLEVER USE OF MAKEUP, HAIRSTYLE, AND ACCESSORIES THESE CAN BE MINIMIZED, TO CREATE THE EFFECT YOU WANT.

Q *I have protruding ears. How can I make sure they don't show?*

A You will need to use your hair to help hide your ears. If you choose to wear your hair up, you will need loose sections of hair falling in front of them. Long hair needs volume at the sides so that your ears are covered, and short hair should be styled with the same aim. Choose a headpiece and veil that are positioned on top of your head.

Q *I have a very high forehead: what are my options for my hair and headpiece?*

A If possible, choose a hairstyle with bangs, which will

**LEFT** *Full or partial bangs with a side part will help disguise a full forehead or a rectangular face.*

immediately disguise your high forehead. You do not want a headdress that adds height, so a wreath (sitting on top of the forehead if you do not have bangs), narrow tiara, or an Alice band will be perfect. Keep your veil close to the top of your head, with volume at the back or sides.

Q *I have very fine hair and need to know how to wear it at my wedding, as well as how to attach a veil and headpiece to it.*

**BELOW** *Wearing your hair long and loose will help conceal protruding ears. Keep earrings minimal in size.*

A If you have long hair, wearing it in a bun will provide volume and give you somewhere to position your headpiece, which can then be used to attach the veil. However, wearing you hair short will give you more headpiece options. These need to grip your head rather than your hair, so selecting a tiara, wreath, or Alice band will give you the base to which to attach your veil.

Q *What can I do to disguise my fairly large nose?*

A Apply a darker shade of foundation all over your nose, then use a highlighter along your cheekbones and on the tip of your chin to bring out these areas. Details and volume at the back of your head will counterbalance your nose. Avoid a center part at all costs.

Q *What do I do to disguise my double chin?*

A Choose an open neckline on the bodice of your dress. Powder your entire neck area with a dark shade of powder or bronzer, and draw attention away from the area by bringing interest and focus to your eyes. Avoid shoulder-length hairstyles and veils.

**ABOVE** *A shrug or jacket will take the emphasis away from particularly prominent collarbones.*

Q *I have very prominent collarbones: what do I do?*

A For a cold-weather wedding, choose a dress with a high collar if you have a long neck. If you have a short neck, make sure you select a neckline that hides your collarbones (see pages 62–63). For a warm-weather wedding, an insert of lace, organza, or other lightweight sheer fabric will camouflage your collarbones. Embellishments, such as beading or embroidery, on the bodice of your dress will distract attention from your upper chest and collarbones.

# wraps, jackets, and coats

YOU MAY FEEL THAT YOU NEED TO COVER UP FOR PART OR ALL OF THE WEDDING. THE VENUE MAY DEMAND THIS, AND IF YOU ARE HAVING A WINTER WEDDING YOU WILL WANT TO KEEP WARM. THE CHOICE DEPENDS ON YOUR PERSONAL PREFERENCE, THE STYLE OF YOUR WEDDING DRESS, AND YOUR BUDGET. FABRICS WILL RANGE FROM FAKE FUR OR VELVET TO LACE AND THE LIGHTEST SHEER FABRICS.

## shrug

A shrug is ideal for wearing during the ceremony if you have chosen a strapless dress or if your upper arms and shoulders are not your best feature.

## bolero

A bolero gives the same coverage as the shrug but is more structured and often a garment in its own right.

## jacket

A jacket is the ideal solution for a cool-weather wedding and allows for the dress shape to be seen and admired.

## coat

A wedding dress with a matching coat is a very elegant solution for winter weddings. Often the coat is embellished and the dress underneath is simpler in style.

## stole

A stole can be made of many different types of fabric, from sheer lace to feathers and fake fur. Make sure that it stays in place as you move around.

## cape

A cape can be short or full length. You could use it as an alternative way of adding color to a winter wedding.

**LEFT** *A fun furry stole will add glamour to your wedding dress.*

**BELOW** *A ribbon lace jacket gives ample coverage while maintaing a sheer look.*

# shoes

BELIEVE IT OR NOT, YOUR CHOICE OF SHOES WILL MAKE YOUR DAY. YOU WILL BE STANDING IN THEM FOR MOST OF THE DAY AND EVENING, AND IF THEY ARE NOT COMFORTABLE IT WILL SHOW ON YOUR FACE.

## style and color

The style of footwear you choose depends on the dress you wear, the venue, and your personality. If you want to take the opportunity to try something unusual, it is often easiest to do so by choosing "different" footwear, whether it's a pair of colorful ballet shoes or pink cowboy boots.

Don't forget to try your dress with your shoes to make sure the length is correct, and practice walking in them while wearing the dress. If you have chosen a colored gown, you can have the shoes dyed to match the dress.

## put comfort first

You may want to select a type of shoe in which you already know how to walk comfortably. If you have never worn a particular style, choose a different one unless you are prepared to practice. Although you may want to wear a stunning pair of stilettos, make sure you have a second pair of more sensible shoes on hand in case your feet give up. Whatever footwear you choose, break it in before the big day. Wear your shoes around the house, scuff the soles, and make sure there are no hard edges that will blister your feet.

**ABOVE** *Remember to test-drive your shoes before the big day.*

**RIGHT** *To add drama, think about wearing a colorful pair of heels—in your colors of course.*

**FAR RIGHT** *Add a little glitz for glamour as you walk down the aisle.*

# the bridal bouquet

YOUR BOUQUET WILL COMPLETE YOUR LOOK AS YOU WALK DOWN THE AISLE, BRINGING TOGETHER YOUR PERSONALITY AND THE COLOR THEME OF YOUR WEDDING. YOU MUST ALSO MAKE SURE THAT THE BOUQUET STYLE COMPLEMENTS YOUR DRESS, BODY SHAPE, AND SCALE.

## making your choice

The range of bouquets available can be overwhelming, but by following the advice given here and overleaf you will be able to select an appropriate and manageable bouquet. Your flowers do not necessarily have to be fresh: silk flowers will provide a lasting memory of your wedding day.

## color

The choice of color for your bouquet needs to harmonize with that of your wedding dress. This can be either tonal or contrasting. See pages 12–17 for the best accent colors for your dominant palette.

## basic shapes

Keep your scale in mind when choosing the size of your bouquet to make sure that the overall look is in proportion.

**Posy** Small, round bouquet that is good for petite brides.

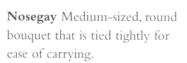

**Nosegay** Medium-sized, round bouquet that is tied tightly for ease of carrying.

**Round** Full bouquet with larger blooms than a nosegay. It is often mixed with some smaller flowers.

### TIP FOR THE DAY
Ask your florist to bind the flower stems to form a handle that you can hold easily.

**Cascade** Tumbling arrangement of flowers that can be of any appropriate length.

**Hand-tied** More informal bouquet, often tied with a ribbon. Also known as a spray.

**Pageant** Bouquet of long-stemmed flowers, often carried over the arm.

**Single** Single "statement" flower. The stem can be ribboned or decorated. Can be decorated with ribbons, bows, or jewels.

**ABOVE** *A floral wristband is a simple yet elegant alternative to a traditional bouquet.*

## style and scale

Your bouquet should tie in with any theme you might have for the day. A relaxed and informal wedding will call for a hand-tied bouquet or even a single flower, while a formal occasion will demand a constructed bouquet such as a nosegay.

The types of flowers you use will also be part of your theme. For example, less formal flowers, such as a hand-tied bouquet with cottage-garden style flowers, will work well for a summer wedding; or choose berries and grasses for a fall ceremony.

Whatever the style or time of year for your wedding, you must also consider your own scale. If you have a petite build, a smaller bouquet with dainty flowers will suit you perfectly; larger, more dramatic blooms will create a balanced look for a grander-scale bride.

## complementing your dress

**Sheath** This simple dress style, best for straight body lines, will benefit from a simple-shaped bouquet such as a hand-tied using only a couple of different flowers in similar tones.

**Empire** With this dress, most of the attention will be on the top half. This gives you the opportunity to hold your bouquet below the bust-line, so a cascade will bring detail to the body of the dress.

**Bias cut** The flowing lines of a bias-cut dress are beautifully enhanced with a pageant-style bouquet or a simple single-stem statement flower.

**Mermaid** With details on the hemline of this dress, a posy or round-style bouquet will draw attention to the waistline.

**A-line** The A-line dress is so versatile that all styles of bouquet will work well.

**Ball gown** To make the most of your wonderful full skirt, make sure the bouquet is the focus of your waist with a nosegay or larger round arrangement.

## completing the picture

If you are having bridesmaids, you may want them to have the same shape bouquet as you, but with different flowers in toning colors. But you can just as easily go for something completely different. Your groom's boutonniere should complement one or two of the flowers in your bouquet.

**RIGHT** *This soft bride's dress is enhanced by carrying some creamy white peonies to coordinate with the white embroidery.*

the bridal party

# bridesmaids' dresses: colors

IT IS AN HONOR TO BE A BRIDESMAID, AND OFTEN THOSE YOU HAVE ASKED WILL BE AS EXCITED AS YOU ARE.
SHOPPING FOR BRIDESMAIDS' OUTFITS CAN BE A FUN EXPERIENCE FOR YOU ALL, ALTHOUGH YOU WILL NEED
A CLEAR IDEA OF WHAT YOU WANT THEM TO LOOK LIKE BECAUSE THEY WILL FRAME YOU IN YOUR WEDDING
PHOTOGRAPHS. HAPPY BRIDESMAIDS MAKE GOOD PHOTOGRAPHS, SO MAKING SURE THEY ARE COMFORTABLE IN
WHAT THEY ARE WEARING WILL GUARANTEE THAT EVERYONE IS RADIANT ON THE DAY.

## colors for all

If you are having only one
bridesmaid, the choice of color
is easier, because you simply
need to choose one that suits
her and complements your color
scheme (see pages 12–17). With
more than one bridesmaid, the
choice can be more challenging.
One might be a redhead,
another a blond, and another
dark-haired: what is going to
suit them all?

It is actually possible to
choose a color that works well
for all your bridesmaids. In the
**colour me beautiful** color
system there are shades that are
universal and will suit everyone,
whatever their coloring.

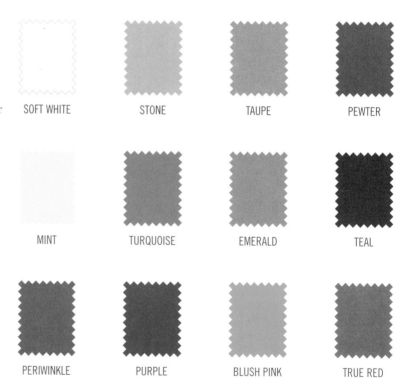

SOFT WHITE    STONE    TAUPE    PEWTER

MINT    TURQUOISE    EMERALD    TEAL

PERIWINKLE    PURPLE    BLUSH PINK    TRUE RED

**ABOVE** *Against the light color of the bridesmaids' dresses, the choice of light flowers blend and balance the overall look.*

**LEFT** *The striking purple of these bridesmaids' dresses is picked out in the bouquets of brightly colored and contrasting flowers.*

# the right shade

The alternative to choosing a universal color is to have a color theme for your bridesmaids, whereby they each wear a shade of the color that suits them best. In this way, you can achieve a stunning look for your bridal party.

The choice of color theme will often be determined by the time of year. Pastels work well in spring or summer, reds and greens in winter. Purples, aquas, and blues will look good all year round.

By following the suggestions opposite you will achieve a colorful and happy group. Selecting colors in this way will also work when you have a mix of adults and children.

**BELOW** *Bridesmaids do not have to wear the same style or color dress, as long as both the shape and the color of their dresses suit them and complement each other.*

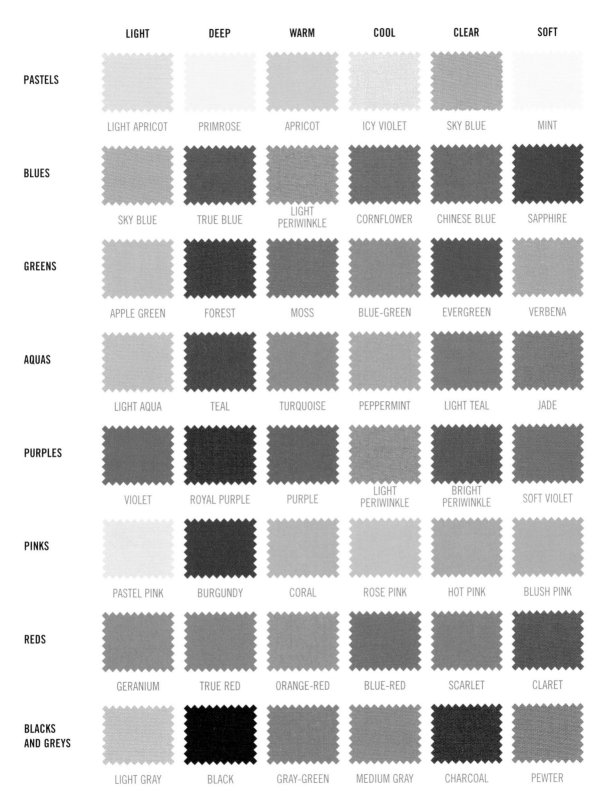

|  | LIGHT | DEEP | WARM | COOL | CLEAR | SOFT |
|---|---|---|---|---|---|---|
| **PASTELS** | LIGHT APRICOT | PRIMROSE | APRICOT | ICY VIOLET | SKY BLUE | MINT |
| **BLUES** | SKY BLUE | TRUE BLUE | LIGHT PERIWINKLE | CORNFLOWER | CHINESE BLUE | SAPPHIRE |
| **GREENS** | APPLE GREEN | FOREST | MOSS | BLUE-GREEN | EVERGREEN | VERBENA |
| **AQUAS** | LIGHT AQUA | TEAL | TURQUOISE | PEPPERMINT | LIGHT TEAL | JADE |
| **PURPLES** | VIOLET | ROYAL PURPLE | PURPLE | LIGHT PERIWINKLE | BRIGHT PERIWINKLE | SOFT VIOLET |
| **PINKS** | PASTEL PINK | BURGUNDY | CORAL | ROSE PINK | HOT PINK | BLUSH PINK |
| **REDS** | GERANIUM | TRUE RED | ORANGE-RED | BLUE-RED | SCARLET | CLARET |
| **BLACKS AND GREYS** | LIGHT GRAY | BLACK | GRAY-GREEN | MEDIUM GRAY | CHARCOAL | PEWTER |

# bridesmaids' dresses: shapes

WHEN YOU START TO THINK ABOUT DRESSES FOR YOUR BRIDESMAIDS, VISIT DEPARTMENT STORES, MALLS, AND LOCAL STORES, AND CHECK THE INTERNET TO GATHER IDEAS AND INSPIRATION. KEEP THEIR SIZES, PERSONALITIES, AND COLORING IN MIND TO MAKE SURE YOU END UP WITH HAPPY AND RELAXED BRIDESMAIDS ON YOUR WEDDING DAY.

## first considerations

You will need to consider the following points:

• If you pay for the bridesmaids' dresses, you will have a lot more say in the matter.

• If the bridesmaids are paying for themselves, let them have their say.

• You may want the dresses to have a life after the wedding, so you will all need to think about whether they can be worn again for other occasions. Choosing an evening dress from a department store will make this more feasible.

• The fabric of the bridesmaids' dresses does not have to be as luxurious as yours. You could even choose the same style dress as yours but in a different fabric, such as cotton.

• You might want a patterned fabric, in which case it is important to keep in mind the scale of your bridesmaids and the size of the pattern.

## one style suits all?

Each of your bridesmaids will, of course, have her own body shape. However, there are certain dress styles that will work well for most women:

**A-line (especially if two-piece)** Because this style of dress comes in many different formats, it will be easier to accommodate all body shapes. The skirt can be fuller or narrower; the waistline on the waist or dropped.

**Empire** This style of dress will suit bridesmaids of any age, especially young girls. It is also comfortable to wear for a long day. This dress can hide a multitude of sins and will work for the unexpected announcement from one of your bridesmaids a few months before the wedding that she is pregnant.

## range of styles

You can still achieve a coordinated group by choosing different dress styles to suit your bridesmaids' respective body shapes (see pages 46–47), but keeping the color the same or choosing a color theme. When making decisions, think about the fact that:

• The bridesmaids' dresses must not be more elaborate than your wedding dress.

• You may want to choose an embellishment to tie in with your dress.

• If you choose a print, make sure the color coordinates with your dress and theme.

**RIGHT** *These bridesmaids stand out in rose pink in the same style dress as the bride.*

## MAKING COMPROMISES

Don't dress your biker friend in a Barbie dress! This doesn't mean that she should come in jeans and motorcycle boots, but a simple style of dress or separates will make her feel more at home. Everyone may have to compromise a little, but some forethought and planning will guarantee that no one is unhappy.

# men's colors

DO NOT OVERLOOK THE MEN WHO WILL BE AT YOUR WEDDING. WHAT THEY CHOOSE (OR YOU TELL THEM) TO WEAR MUST COMPLEMENT WHAT YOU ARE WEARING AND BE CONSISTENT WITH THE REST OF THE BRIDAL PARTY. A LITTLE GUIDANCE ON COLOR AND FIT WILL ENSURE THAT THEY, TOO, LOOK GOOD AND FEEL COMFORTABLE.

## light

His look is pale and youthful, and he may even have sensitive skin. His beard is light and his hair blond or minimal. He has blond eyebrows and lashes, and his eyes are pale blue, gray, or pale green.

Don't overwhelm him with very dark colors: charcoal grays and light navy are best. If he has to wear dark colors, make sure his tie/ascot is in a light color.

## deep

His look is strong and definite. He has dark brown to black hair, and his facial hair is dark and prominent. His skin can be pale, through olive, to the darkest brown. He has deep, dark eyes.

Keep his colors strong and deep. A shirt in a contrasting color is also good.

## warm

He has an overall golden look consisting of reddish-blond, auburn, or red hair. His skin is pale with freckles and his beard may grow in reddish. His eyes are green, blue, or brown, perhaps with yellow flecks in them.

Charcoal gray and navy are much better for him than black. Choose his shirt color carefully: white will make him look as if he has been up all night, so go for soft white or cream.

## cool

His hair may be graying at the temples or completely gray, while his facial hair may be black with flecks of gray or white. He has rosy or pink tones to his skin if he is Caucasian, and a bluish-gray undertone if he is African American. His eyes are blue, gray, or cool brown.

Black works well, teamed with blues, pinks, lavenders, and even burgundy. Avoid any browns or yellow-based colors.

## clear

He has dark hair and bright, clear eyes that can be green, blue, or brown. His complexion is often pale with dark eyebrows and lashes.

Because of his contrasting look he needs bright, clear colors to complement his striking appearance. Fabrics with a sheen work well as they reflect the light. Contrast his look between dark and light or bright colors.

## muted

He has dark blond to medium brown hair with eyebrows and lashes to match. His skin is light to olive with soft, blended tones in his eyes, which can be blue, green, or brown.

He needs to avoid high contrast and is much better in a blended, tonal look—woven, textured fabrics are perfect. Shantung ties and ascots work best. Avoid harsh contrasts: charcoal gray and soft white will be far more flattering than black and pure white.

# men's body shapes

GETTING THE RIGHT SUIT OR OUTFIT FOR YOUR PARTNER IS NEARLY AS IMPORTANT AS CHOOSING YOUR OWN
DRESS. IT'S NOT JUST A MATTER OF PURCHASING A SMART SUIT: MEN'S SUITS COME IN DIFFERENT SHAPES AND
CUTS, SO IT IS IMPORTANT TO UNDERSTAND WHAT HIS BEST STYLE WILL BE. WHAT THE GROOM WEARS WILL
DICTATE THE LOOK FOR THE REST OF THE MEN IN THE BRIDAL PARTY.

## take a look

This is the fun part. Get your man to strip down in front of you and take a good look at him. His body shape will dictate the best looks for him, whether it's the shape of his suit, the type of fabric, or the pattern on his tie. You may also need to consider his proportions. For example, a man with short legs does not look good in wide trousers, while tapered trousers will make a long-legged man look like a beanpole.

## check the fit

• The collar of the jacket should fit against the collar of the shirt with no gap in between.
• Jacket sleeves should end at the break of the wrist, allowing ¾ inch (1.5 cm) of shirt to show below the jacket sleeve.
• For a good fit the waistband of the trousers should sit as close to the navel as possible.
• The trouser legs should fall with one break only across the shoe.

**BELOW** *Details such as real button-holes on jackets, double cuffs, and cufflinks all add to the glamour of the day.*

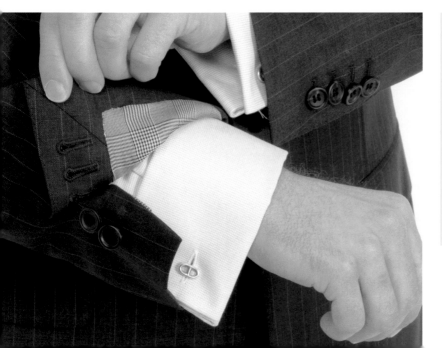

## BUY OR RENT?

Keep in mind whether this is going to be an outfit worn just once or something your partner will be able to wear for other occasions. To invest in an expensive suit when his usual working wardrobe consists of casual wear is not wise. If this is the case, consider renting (and fitting) a suit.

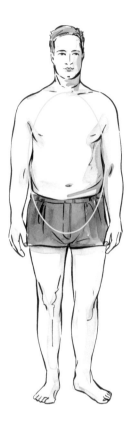

## inverted triangle

Broad shoulders narrowing down to the hips. Any Italian styling, with its wide lapels and shoulder lines will enhance his body shape—don't hide his athletic silhouette. Choose a crisp, lightweight fabric; any patterns should be geometric or striped. If he is short in the leg, make sure that his pants are not too wide.

## rectangle

Shoulders and hips in line with each other. Standard single- or double-breasted British-cut suits will work well if your groom has this body shape—make sure the jacket is slightly waisted—as will all formal wear. Just check his proportions and make sure his jacket sits well against his shirt collar and that the sleeves are the right length.

## round

Rounded shoulder line and fuller stomach. The fabric of his outfit needs to be soft to guarantee the correct fit across the chest and stomach. If he has a particularly full stomach and his trousers tend to slip below it, consider persuading him into wearing a vest to give a smooth and contoured look to his shape.

# men's outfits

THERE ARE DIFFERENT STYLES OF FORMAL WEDDING ATTIRE FOR MEN, SOME OF WHICH ARE MORE TRADITIONAL THAN OTHERS. WHATEVER THE STYLE, IF YOU WEAR A LONG WEDDING GOWN, THE MEN'S SUITS SHOULD BE WORN WITH A FORMAL SHIRT AND TIE.

## formal styles

**Tails (morning dress)** This is the most formal suit worn during the day and works well for all body shapes and sizes. It is available in black or charcoal worn with pinstripe trousers or gray worn with matching trousers.

**Tuxedo (black tie)** Another formal look for weddings held later in the day and for evening receptions. The suit can be either single- or double-breasted. Choose notched lapels for inverted triangle and rectangle body shapes, shawl lapels for round. For a less formal look, you have the option of adding a colored tie and vest or cummerbund.

**RIGHT** *This classic tailcoat is given an updated look with a fashionable silk vest and matching tie.*

**Frock coat** A recent popular addition to the wedding scene, the frock coat can be made of luxury fabrics such as brocade or velvet. It looks best on average to tall inverted triangle and rectangle body shapes, but can be worn with a vest by a tall, round man.

**Suit** This is the most relaxed of formal wear and is appropriate for any time of day. If the men aren't used to wearing suits during the day, this might be their most comfortable option. Choose fabrics carefully: a crisper fabric for an inverted triangle, lightweight worsted for a rectangle, and a softer, woven fabric such as lightweight flannel for a round body shape.

## alternatives

If a uniform is part of your groom's life, he may wear the formal version of it for your wedding. The same applies if he has a traditional dress, religious or otherwise. For an informal wedding, you may want him in a suit, with or without a tie. A tropical wedding calls for a white dinner jacket.

## on show too

Whether you want the best man, fathers, and groomsmen (ushers) to dress the same as the groom is entirely a personal choice. However, the best man usually wears the same style of suit as the groom. What the other men in the bridal party wear often depends on the formality of the wedding.

If you choose to have a ring bearer, just make sure that he is comfortable in what he wears to avoid any last-minute tantrums.

**ABOVE** *The formality of the black tie has been given a wedding makeover with a silk vest and tie.*

## RENTAL

Don't hesitate to rent the men's attire, but make sure that they have all tried their suits on in advance and that sleeve lengths are correct and trousers fit properly.

# men's accessories

THE WAY THE MEN IN THE BRIDAL PARTY WEAR THE VARIOUS ACCESSORIES THAT COMPLETE THEIR OUTFIT IS IMPORTANT, AND YOU WILL WANT TO MAKE SURE THEY GET IT RIGHT. THIS IS WHERE YOU CAN COORDINATE OR CONTRAST COLORS, AND ALLOW THE GROOM TO DEMONSTRATE SOME OF HIS PERSONALITY.

## shirts, ties and cuff links

The choice of shirt will depend on the choice of neckwear:

**Tie** A standard tie requires a standard shirt collar.

**Self-tie ascot** This can be worn with a standard or wing collar.

**Ascot** An ascot dictates a wing collar to go with it.

**Bow tie** Team this with a standard or wing collar. Whatever the type of neckwear, it must be made from silk so that it falls well.

**Cuff links** These are only worn with a shirt that has French (double) fold-back cuffs. Beware of choosing jokey, inappropriate cuff links for a formal wedding.

**LEFT** *A color-coordinated vest and tie turn a suit into something special.*

## vests

You can choose a vest in the same color as the jacket, or a contrasting one. Consider having the groom wear something different from the rest of the men in order for him to stand out and make his own fashion statement! With any vests, always leave the lowest button open.

## cummerbunds, belts, and suspenders

A cummerbund can be worn with a tuxedo and is great for tidying up the waistline and disguising a rounded stomach. A cummerbund should always be teamed with a bow tie, and you can have fun choosing a suitable color for both.

If the suit trousers have loops, these call for a belt (and certainly no suspenders). If the suit is rented and cannot be altered to fit for the occasion, and there are no belt loops, suspenders will be needed.

Under no circumstances should any of these three be worn together.

## grooming

Just like you, your partner needs to think about his grooming ahead of time.

Make sure he has booked a haircut that will look just right in time for the photographs. If he has heavy eyebrows, they should be controlled—you may need to get out your tweezers. It goes without saying that shaving or beard trimming must be attended to at the appropriate time prior to the ceremony. The groom's hands will also be on display on the day, so treat him to a manicure the day before the wedding or do it yourself if you have time.

## shoes and socks

Black shoes should be highly polished and not scuffed; black patent can be worn with a tuxedo. Make sure any labels on the soles of the shoes are removed before wearing.

Socks should be worn in plain, dark colors and made of wool, cotton, or silk. Avoid man-made fibers to prevent discomfort. They should be long enough to cover the lower calf.

**ABOVE** *A colorful boutonniere easily co-ordinates with the rest of the bridal party.*

## boutonnieres

A boutonniere is a small flower arrangement for the buttonhole. Your groom's boutonniere should relate in variety of flowers and/or color to your own bouquet.

Boutonnieres for the rest of the men in the bridal party should be in the style or color of the groom's, but not exactly the same in other respects. Make sure that the stem of the boutonniere is securely pinned to the lapel.

# mothers' outfits

YOUR WEDDING DAY IS ALSO A MOMENTOUS ONE IN YOUR MOTHER'S LIFE, AND YOUR FUTURE MOTHER-IN-LAW'S,
TOO. YOU WILL WANT THEM TO BE HAPPY AND RELAXED ON THE DAY, AND WHAT THEY WEAR IS VERY MUCH PART
OF HOW THEY WILL FEEL—NOT TO MENTION LOOKING GOOD IN THE PHOTOGRAPHS!

## fitting in

Both mothers should wait
until you have selected your
own dress and those of your
bridesmaids before choosing
their own, so that they too can
feel part of the bridal party and
neither under- nor overdressed.

## colors

The mothers may want to bring
some of your color theme into
their own outfits, perhaps in a
trim, an accessory, or even a
corsage. What you want to avoid
is a kaleidoscope of colors made
up of your dress, your
bridesmaids' and the mothers'—
unless that is specifically the
effect you are trying to create.

For more detailed advice
on colors, see pages 12–17.

**RIGHT** *This three-piece outfit
coordinates with the hat and colorful
shoes for a special event.*

looking great on
your big day

# bridal lingerie

THIS IS THE DAY ON WHICH SPECIAL UNDERWEAR IS CALLED FOR. DON'T JUST RUSH OUT AND BUY A NEW SET OF THE THINGS YOU NORMALLY WEAR: YOUR LINGERIE NEEDS TO WORK WITH THE STYLE OF WEDDING DRESS YOU ARE GOING TO WEAR. DO NOT BE SHY ABOUT TAKING ADVICE FROM THE PROFESSIONALS.

## colors and textures

Check how fine or translucent the fabric of your dress is before choosing embellished, lacy underwear. Flesh-colored lingerie shows far less through whites or creams than pure white, which will stand out against your skin, particularly if you are tanned. With other wedding dress colors, have fun coordinating the shades.

## bras

You will need to be measured properly before you buy a bra. Brand sizes vary, and you will even find that different bra shapes call for different-sized cups. Once properly fitted, your bra will be comfortable yet give you support, so there should

**RIGHT** *Every bride deserves beautiful underwear under her dress.*

be no need for you to tug, pull, or fidget with it on the day.

If you are wearing a corset- or bustier-style bodice, you may not need any additional support since the garment is fitted to you. You may want to wear a bustier under your dress, so make sure it is comfortable and there are no bones or wiring cutting into you, especially when you sit down.

If your wedding dress has sleeves, you might want to have little ribbons sewn in on the shoulders to prevent your bra straps from wandering.

## panties

No Visible Pantie Line, please. You may be tempted to put yourself into "magic" high-control underpants—just make sure you have worn them ahead of time and are comfortable with what they do to your body. A good alternative is an all-in-one body shaper. If your dress is sheer and you feel comfortable in bikini-style panties or a thong, these can provide the solution to a VPL.

Whatever you choose, make sure you are able to answer nature's calls easily.

## hosiery

Brides are often tempted to wear hold-ups or stockings on their wedding day rather than panty hose, which do not have much sex appeal. If you go for stockings and your skirt is slim-fitting, make sure the clasps on your garter belt are covered with ribbon.

If you have chosen open shoes, make sure you wear sandalfoot hosiery.

## petticoats

The style of your dress will dictate what petticoat, if any, you need to wear in order for it to fall properly. For example, a ballgown style will invariably come with layers and layers of petticoats, while an A-line dress may need one to stiffen up the line a little, if that is the look you are after.

The supplier of your dress will be able to show you a variety of petticoats best suited to your dress. Sheaths or empire-line dresses are unlikely to need petticoats as they should already be fully lined. If they are not, you will need a simple slip under the dress to make sure it hangs without clinging.

**ABOVE** *Wearing the right underwear will guarantee that you are comfortable all day long.*

## TIPS FOR THE DAY

Try the complete set of underwear with your dress to make sure there is no show-through, VPL, or other unsightly lumps and bumps. Wear the underwear for a day to make certain it is practical and comfortable, whether you're standing up or sitting down.

# getting ready

WHETHER YOU ARE A MAKEUP AFICIONADO OR HAVE NEVER TOUCHED THE STUFF, ON YOUR WEDDING DAY YOU MUST BE PREPARED TO MAKE SOME CHANGES TO YOUR STANDARD ROUTINE. YOUR MAKEUP WILL NEED TO LAST FOR THE DURATION OF THE EVENT, SO SPECIAL APPLICATION MAY BE NECESSARY. YOU MAY CHOOSE TO HAVE YOUR MAKEUP DONE FOR YOU—JUST MAKE SURE YOUR GROOM WILL RECOGNIZE YOU AS YOU WALK DOWN THE AISLE. REHEARSING HOW YOU WILL LOOK ON THE DAY IS A MUST.

## application techniques

A good skincare routine is essential and should have started some months before the wedding. On the day, make sure you allow enough time before the photographer arrives to apply your makeup or to have it applied.

**Skin** Prepare your skin with a primer, which helps even out your complexion and ensure that your foundation lasts longer. Apply foundation with a sponge or brush, working one area at a time rather than dotting it around. Next, if necessary, apply concealer to hide any blemishes or dark circles. Using a large powder puff or cotton, powder your entire face, avoiding the eye area, and then powder again.

The layers will give a long-lasting finish to your makeup. Remove any excess with a powder brush.

**Eyes** Use an eye base on your eyelids to prevent your eye shadow from creasing. Apply mascara generously, leaving time for it to dry between coats and concentrating on the outer edge—on your wedding day, waterproof mascara is a must. Use a pencil if your eyebrows require definition.

**Lips** Lip base forms the perfect starting point for your lip color application, which should be followed by lip pencil. Apply lipstick/gloss with a lip brush. Use a single layer of tissue over the lips and then powder over with your brush. Finally, gently spray your whole face with a fine water mist.

**ABOVE** *Layering your lipstick will guarantee a long-lasting finish.*

# light makeup colors

THE OVERALL LOOK OF YOUR MAKEUP WILL BE LIGHT AND DELICATE, SO DO NOT OVERPOWER IT WITH STRONG, DARK SHADES FOR EITHER EYE SHADOWS OR LIPSTICK.

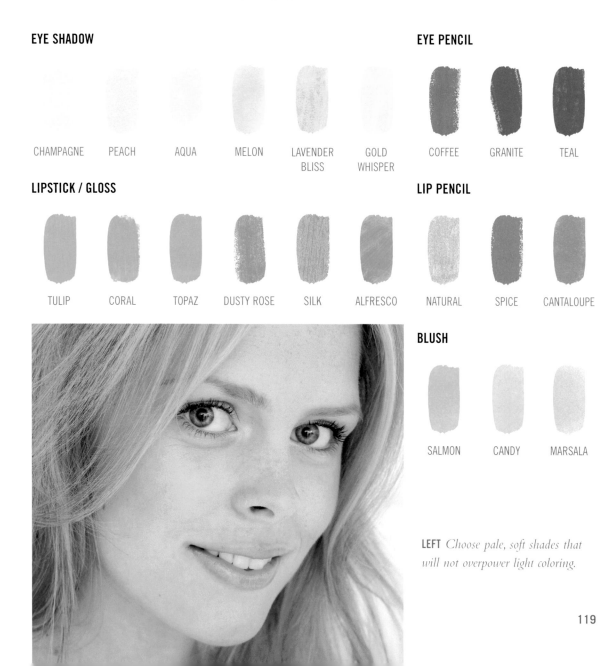

### EYE SHADOW

| CHAMPAGNE | PEACH | AQUA | MELON | LAVENDER BLISS | GOLD WHISPER |
| --- | --- | --- | --- | --- | --- |

### EYE PENCIL

| COFFEE | GRANITE | TEAL |
| --- | --- | --- |

### LIPSTICK / GLOSS

| TULIP | CORAL | TOPAZ | DUSTY ROSE | SILK | ALFRESCO |
| --- | --- | --- | --- | --- | --- |

### LIP PENCIL

| NATURAL | SPICE | CANTALOUPE |
| --- | --- | --- |

### BLUSH

| SALMON | CANDY | MARSALA |
| --- | --- | --- |

**LEFT** *Choose pale, soft shades that will not overpower light coloring.*

# deep makeup colors

ALTHOUGH YOUR COLORING IS DEEP, ON YOUR WEDDING DAY YOUR MAKEUP NEEDS TO BE A LITTLE LIGHTER THAN YOU WOULD NORMALLY WEAR. GO FOR STRONG EYES AND LIGHTER LIPS OR VICE VERSA.

## EYE SHADOW

| APRICOT | TOFFEE | COCOA | HEATHER | KHAKI | BAY LEAF |
| --- | --- | --- | --- | --- | --- |

## EYE PENCIL

| SOFT BLACK | PETROL | BROWN |
| --- | --- | --- |

## LIPSTICK / GLOSS

| KAZZBAR | MAHOGANY | RUBY | RUM | SAVANNAH | TAMARIND |
| --- | --- | --- | --- | --- | --- |

## LIP PENCIL

| RED | RUSSET | SPICE |
| --- | --- | --- |

## BLUSH

| COGNAC | PORT | MUSCAT |
| --- | --- | --- |

**RIGHT** *Defining eyes with a pencil gives a dramatic look for a deep bride's coloring.*

# warm makeup colors

WHEN CHOOSING YOUR MAKEUP COLORS, THINK GOLDEN, COPPER, BRONZE, AND AMBER. MAKE SURE THE SHINE AND GLITTER ARE KEPT TO A MINIMUM SO THAT THE PHOTOGRAPHER'S FLASH DOESN'T REFLECT TOO MUCH.

## EYE SHADOW

PEACH    TANGERINE    GOLD WHISPER    GRAYED GREEN    TOFFEE    KHAKI

## EYE PENCIL

MOSS    OLIVE    BROWN

## LIPSTICK / GLOSS

SORBET    TERRA-COTTA    SPICED PEACH    NUTMEG    TANGERINE    WARM SAND

## LIP PENCIL

SPICE    RUSSET    CANTALOUPE

## BLUSH

COGNAC    ALMOND    SALMON

**LEFT** *All this warm bride's makeup shades have a hint of gold or yellow in them.*

# cool makeup colors

YOUR ROSY COMPLEXION AND COOL EYES WILL BE COMPLEMENTED BY COOL SHADES. BLENDING YOUR EYE SHADOWS TOGETHER WILL GUARANTEE THAT YOUR EYES SHINE THROUGHOUT THE DAY.

## EYE SHADOW

OPAL  PEARL  MERCURY  DELFT  DUSK  HEATHER

## EYE PENCIL

MARINE  AMETHYST  GRANITE

## LIPSTICK / GLOSS

BONBON  CERISE  SOFT MAUVE  PINK SHELL  FUCHSIA  SANGRIA

## LIP PENCIL

ROSE  POSY  NATURAL

## BLUSH

ROSE  PORT  CANDY

**RIGHT** *Soft pink lipstick and blush bring out the color in this cool bride's eyes.*

# clear makeup colors

BRIGHT, CLEAR COLORS AS EITHER LIPSTICK OR EYE SHADOW ARE A MUST TO CREATE YOUR WEDDING MAKEUP. JUST LIKE YOU, IT MUST BE STRIKING.

## EYE SHADOW

| CHAMPAGNE | PEPPERMINT | STEEL | LAGOON | INDIAN OCEAN | TANGERINE |

## EYE PENCIL

| PETROL | AMETHYST | SOFT BLACK |

## LIPSTICK / GLOSS

| WARM PINK | FIESTA | STRAWBERRY | MANGO | ALFRESCO | CORAL |

## LIP PENCIL

| RED | CANTALOUPE | POSY |

## BLUSH

| SIENNA | MUSCAT | MARSALA |

**LEFT** *This clear bride's stunning blue eyes are perfectly complemented by a bright lipstick.*

# soft makeup colors

YOUR GENTLE, SOFT EYES SHOULD NOT BE OVERPOWERED BY BRIGHT-COLORED SHADOWS AND PENCILS. DO NOT FORGET THAT IF YOUR EYEBROWS ARE BLOND THEY MAY REQUIRE A LITTLE DEFINITION.

## EYE SHADOW

| MELON | FAWN | PEWTER | SMOKE | INDIAN OCEAN | LILAC |
|-------|------|--------|-------|--------------|-------|

## EYE PENCIL

| COCOA | MOSS | EGGPLANT |
|-------|------|----------|

## LIPSTICK / GLOSS

| SANDALWOOD | SOFT MAUVE | BREEZE | NUDE | WARM SAND | PINK SHELL |
|------------|------------|--------|------|-----------|------------|

## LIP PENCIL

| NATURAL | SPICE | ROSE |
|---------|-------|------|

## BLUSHER

| SIENNA | ROSE | MUSCAT |
|--------|------|--------|

**RIGHT** *Blended smoky eyes work wonderfully well with natural-toned lipstick for this soft bride.*

# final word

IT WILL FEEL AS IF THERE ARE A MILLION THINGS TO THINK ABOUT WHEN YOU PLAN YOUR WEDDING. SOME CAN BE PLANNED WELL IN ADVANCE, OTHERS WILL HAVE TO BE DEALT WITH A WEEK BEFORE OR EVEN ON THE DAY.

## grooming

Your grooming schedule should begin two to three months before the big day. By the time your wedding arrives you should have established a good skincare routine, your body should be waxed, and, if necessary, eyebrows should have been shaped and tinted, as well as your eyelashes. Treat yourself to a couple of pedicures and manicures before the day.

## if you wear glasses

You may want to consider styles that will fit in well with what you are wearing. If you choose a traditional white dress, dark-framed glasses will overpower the look—rimless glasses or half frames are better. Nonreflective lenses will guarantee that your eyes are seen through the lens rather than the flash of the camera bulb.

**RIGHT** *Careful preparation will guarantee that you look your best when the day finally arrives.*

## emergency kit

Someone in the bridal party will need to take charge of an emergency kit, which should contain a spare pair of panty hose/stockings as well as Band-Aids (in case you haven't broken in your shoes properly). An emery board and spare needle and thread might also be useful. Don't forget indigestion tablets, headache pills, and tissues.

You should also entrust somone with your makeup bag, which should contain powder, mascara, lip pencil, and lipstick/gloss to refresh your look during the day.

## good photography

Remember that shimmer and shine in your makeup will grab the light for color photography, so make sure you keep your makeup matte. Don't forget to eat *before* you start the final countdown to applying your makeup and getting dressed, and it's best to drink through a straw before the ceremony.

You will be asked to smile a thousand times on your wedding day, so a trip to the dental hygienist a week or so before will give you a beaming smile all day.

*Have a wonderful wedding day!*

# index

Page numbers in italics refer
to illustrations.

## A

A-line style *23*, *43*, *43*, *57*, 100
  bouquets for 92
accent colors 12–17

## B

ball gown *43*, *43*, *51*, *66*
  bouquets for 92
beiges, to suit complexion 26–9
bias-cut style *42*, 43, 49
  bouquets for 92
blacks, for wedding dress 37, *37*
blues, for wedding dress 32–3,
  *32–3*
bodices 60, *61*
body shapes
  dress styles for 48–59
  men's 104–5, *105*
  outfits for 68–71
  women's 46–7
bolero 88
bouquets 90–2, *90–1*, *93*
boutonnieres 109
bracelets 83
bridesmaids' dresses
  colors 96–8, *96–9*
  shapes 100
brocade 45

## C

cape 88
chiffon 45
chin, double, disguising 87
city chic style 41
classic style 41
clear coloring
  accent colors 16
  colors for 16, 18, 22, 24, 26, 29
  makeup colors *123*
  men 103
coats 88
  styles 68
collarbones, prominent 87

## color

  elements 11
  importance of 10–11
  to suit complexion 10, 12–29
column body shape 47
  dress styles for 56
complexion, color types 11
cool coloring
  accent colors 15
  colors for 15, 18, 20, 22, 25, 26
  makeup colors *122*
  men 103
Cornwall, Duchess of *15*
creams, to suit complexion 22–5
creative style 40

## D

damask 45
deep coloring
  accent colors 13
  colors for 13, 18, 20, 22, 26, 28
  makeup colors *120*
  men 102
dramatic style 40
dresses
  styles 70
  vintage 70, *70*
  *see also* bridesmaids' dresses;
    wedding dresses
duchess satin 45
dupioni 45

## E

earrings 83
ears, protruding 86
embellishments 45
emergency kit 125
empire style *19*, 42–3, *42*, *53*, 100
  bouquets for 92

## F

fabrics 44–5
face shapes 76–7
  hairstyles to suit 78–82
fascinators 113, *113*
Ferguson, Sarah *14*

flapper dress *70*
forehead, high 86–7
frock coat 107

## G

georgette 45
glasses 125
greens, for wedding dress 30–1,
  *30–1*
grooming 125

## H

hair, fine 87
hats, mother's 112–13, *112*
headpieces 84–5, *84*
Holmes, Katie *41*
hosiery 117
hourglass body shape 46
  dress styles for 48, 50
Hurley, Liz *16*

## J

jackets 88
  styles 68
jewelry 83
Jonsson, Ulrika *12*

## L

lace, types 45
light coloring
  accent colors 12
  colors for 12, 18, 22, 24, 26, 28
  makeup colors *119*
  men 102
lingerie 116–17, *116*, *117*
Lopez, Jennifer *13*

## M

makeup 118–24
  application techniques 118
  colors 119–24
men 102–9
  accessories 108–9
  body shapes 104–5, *105*
  colors for 102–3
  grooming 109

outfits 106–7, *106, 107*
    checking fit 104
    to suit body shape 105
mermaid style *23*, 43, *43, 55*
    bouquets for 92
metallics, for wedding dress 37, *37*
moiré 45
mother
    hats 112–13, *112, 113*
    outfits 110–11, *110, 111*
mother-to-be, dress styles for 58
muted coloring, men 103

**N**
natural style 41
necklaces 83
necklines 62, *63*
nose, large, disguising 87

**O**
organza 45
oval face 77
    hairstyles for 78

**P**
pants, styles 71
pantsuit 71
page boys 107
photography, make-up for 125
pinks, pastels, for wedding dress 34, *34*
pregnancy, dress styles for 58
proportions 47
purples, for wedding dress 36, *36*

**R**
rectangle body shape 47
    dress styles for 58
    men's 105, *105*
rectangle face shape 77
    hairstyles for 80
reds, for wedding dress 35, *35*
renting outfits 104, 107
ring bearers 107
rings 83
romantic style 41

round body shape, men's 105, *105*
round face 77
    hairstyles for 82

**S**
scale 47
shantung silk 45
shapes
    body 46–7
    dress styles for 48–59
    men's 104–5, *105*
    face 76–7
        hairstyles to suit 78–82
sheath dress 42, *42, 59*
    bouquets for 92
shoes 89
    men's 109
shrugs *23, 64*, 88
silk crepe 45
skincare 118, 125
skirts, styles 69
sleeves 64, *65*
soft coloring
    accent colors 17
    colors for 17, 18, 21, 22, 25, 26
    makeup colors *124*
square face 77
    hairstyles for 79
Stefani, Gwen *40*
stole 88, *88*
strapless dress *27*
suit *69*
suits, men's 107

**T**
taffeta 45
tails (morning dress) 106, *106*
teals, for wedding dress 33, *33*
trains 66, *67*
triangle body shape 46
    dress styles for 52
    inverted 47
    dress shapes for 54
    men's 105, *105*
triangle face shape
    inverted 77

hairstyles for 81
tuxedo (black tie) outfit 106, 107

**U**
uniform 107

**V**
veils 85, *85*
velvet 45
vests 109

**W**
waistlines 60, *61*
warm coloring
    accent colors 14
    colors for 14, 18, 21, 22, 26, 29
    makeup colors *121*
    men 102
watches 83
wedding dresses
    alternative outfits 68–71
    colors 10, 11, 26–37
    details 60–7
    embellishments 45
    fabrics 44–5
    planning 72
    scale and proportion 47
    shapes 42–3
    shopping for 72–3
    styles 40–3
    trying on 73
Wessex, Countess of *17*
whites, to suit complexion 18–21
wraps 88

**Z**
Zellweger, Renée *41*

# acknowledgments

This book would not have seen the light of day without Chris Scarles thinking about 350,000 brides whose first thought after the proposal is what they are going to wear.

The Hamlyn team was totally supportive and fun to work with. Jasmine, gardenia, and orchid whites now hold no secrets for them.

The critical input of Louise Ravenscroft on the first draft was, as ever, much appreciated.

Christine Southam was particularly generous in handing over her wedding treasure case complete with Ian Stuart dress, while Rose Southam's bridesmaid paraphernalia was also shared with us. Ancilla McPherson also kindly lent us her wedding dress.

Audrey Sirian (just married) advised us on what a bride-to-be would be looking for in this book. Thank you to her photographer, Kelsy Nielson.

The colour me beautiful head office team of Rosalie Poels (newly engaged) and Fiona Wellins were as helpful as usual in organizing the dresses and accessories; both are now experts at ironing wedding dresses. Thanks too to Georgina Scarles and Sophie Scarles for their help on the busy photo shoot.

Even though we've both been married for some decades, this book brought back many lovely memories. We wish all the brides-to-be and their mothers as much fun as we have had in writing this bridal manual.

Pat Henshaw & Veronique Henderson

**Executive Editor** Katy Denny
**Senior Editor** Charlotte Macey
**Executive Art Editor** Penny Stock
**Designer** Geoff Borin
**Senior Production Controller**
Amanda Mackie
**Picture Research**
Zoë Spilberg

## Picture acknowledgments

Special photography: © Octopus Publishing Group Limited/Vanessa Davies.

Other photography: Alamy Ace Stock Ltd. 71, Chris Rout/Bubbles Photolibrary 72, i love images 103 center, Image Source Black 98, Jupiter Images/Brand X 92, Ron Chapple Stock 73, Sean Bolton 109, Stockbyte 58; Corbis Elisa Lazo de Valdez 70, Pool Photography 15, Reuters 13, Richard T. Nowicz 97 below; Favourbrook Menswear, London 107, 108; Getty Images Andersen Ross/Stockbyte 118, ColorBlind Images 4, Comstock 102 center, Harald Eisenberger 117, Hitoshi Nishimura 55, Ryan McVay 101, Stephen Wallis 89 above, Stockbyte 102 right; Etiquette at Austin Reed 106; Hats By Sherry www.hatsbysherry.co.uk 112; IPC Syndication all 90-91; istockphoto.com iofoto 103 left; Johanna Hehir 49; photo by Kelsy Nielson 83; Masterfile 97 above; Octopus Publishing Group Mike Prior 104; PA Photos 17, James Whatling/UK Press 40 right, Pressens 12, Robert Evans/AP 41 right; Photolibrary VStock 102 left; Punchstock 125, DAJ 51; Rex Features 14, Action Press 16, Sipa Press 41 left; SuperStock Anton Vengo 103 right; Tips Images Ltd. Bildagentur 11, Juice Images 113, Photononstop 116; Vera Mont 69 www.veramont.com

---

Many thanks to the following for providing dressses, shoes, flowers and accessories for the photo shoot:

### DRESSES
alfredangelo.com
bhs.co.uk
foreverbridal.com
ianstuart-bride.com
motasem.co.uk
pronovias.com

### SHOES
victoriaallinson.co.uk
lkbennett.co.uk

### FLOWERS
Georgie Bailey Floral Design:
www.gbfd.co.uk

### ACCCESSORIES
Luellasboudoir.co.uk
Yarwood-white.com

Please contact Colour Me Beautiful for more information on services, products and how to become a consultant:

**UK and Headquarters for Europe, Africa and the Middle East**
66 The Business Centre,
15–17 Ingate Place,
London SW8 3NS
www.colourmebeautiful.co.uk
info@cmb.co.uk
+44 (0)20 7627 5211

**China**
www.qixincolor.com
**Finland**
www.colourmebeautiful.fi
**Ireland**
www.cmbireland.com
**Hong Kong**
www.colourmebeautiful.hk

**Netherlands, Germany & Belgium**
www.colourmebeautiful.nl
**Norway**
www.colour-me-beautiful.no
**Portugal**
www.cmb.com.pt
**Slovenia**
www.cmb.si
**South Africa**
www.colormebeautiful.co.za
**Spain**
www.colormebeautiful.es
**Sweden**
www.colormebeautiful.se
**USA**
www.colormebeautiful.com